The Revolt of the Masses

by JOSE ORTEGA Y GASSET

THE REVOLT OF THE MASSES
MAN AND PEOPLE
MAN AND CRISIS
WHAT IS PHILOSOPHY?
MEDITATIONS ON QUIXOTE
HISTORY AS A SYSTEM

JOSE ORTEGA Y GASSET

THE
REVOLT OF
THE MASSES

AUTHORIZED TRANSLATION FROM THE SPANISH

W. W. NORTON & COMPANY
NEW YORK • LONDON

The Spanish original, "Le Rebelión de las Masas," was
published in 1930

This translation, authorised by Sr. Ortega y Gasset, remains
anonymous at the translator's request

First published as a Norton paperback 1964
Reissued 1993

ISBN 0-393-31095-7

W. W. Norton & Company, Inc.
500 Fifth Avenue, New York, N.Y. 10110
www.wwnorton.com

W. W. Norton & Company Ltd.
15 Carlisle Street, London W1D 3BS

PRINTED IN THE UNITED STATES OF AMERICA

20 21 22 23 24

Contents

Prefatory Note

In my book *España Invertebrada,* published in 1922, in an article in *El Sol* entitled "Masas" (1926), and in two lectures given to the Association of Friends of Art in Buenos Aires (1928), I have treated the subject developed in the present essay. My purpose now is to collect and complete what I have already said, so as to produce an organic doctrine concerning the most important fact of our time.

The Revolt of the Masses

1

The Coming of the Masses

THERE is one fact which, whether for good or ill, is of utmost importance in the public life of Europe at the present moment. This fact is the accession of the masses to complete social power. As the masses, by definition, neither should nor can direct their own personal existence, and still less rule society in general, this fact means that actually Europe is suffering from the greatest crisis that can afflict peoples, nations, and civilisation. Such a crisis has occurred more than once in history. Its characteristics and its consequences are well known. So also is its name. It is called the rebellion of the masses. In order to understand this formidable fact, it is important from the start to avoid giving to the words "rebellion," "masses," and "social power" a meaning exclusively or primarily political. Public life is not solely political, but equally, and even primarily, intellectual, moral, economic, religious; it comprises all our collective habits, including our fashions both of dress and of amusement.

Perhaps the best line of approach to this historical phenomenon may be found by turning our attention to a visual experience, stressing one aspect of our epoch which is plain to our very eyes. This fact is quite simple to enunciate, though not so to analyse. I shall call it the fact of agglomeration, of "plenitude." Towns are full of people, houses full of tenants, hotels full of guests, trains full of travellers, cafés full of customers, parks full of promenaders, consulting-rooms of famous doctors full of patients, theatres full of spectators, and beaches full of bathers. What previously was, in general, no problem, now begins to be an everyday one, namely, to find room.

That is all. Can there be any fact simpler, more patent, more constant in actual life? Let us now pierce the plain surface of this observation and we shall be surprised to see how there wells forth an unexpected spring in which the white light of day, of our actual day, is broken up into its rich chromatic content. What is it that we see, and the sight of which causes us so much surprise? We see the multitude, as such, in possession of the places and the instruments created by civilisation. The slightest re-flection will then make us surprised at our own surprise. What about it? Is this not the ideal state of things? The theatre has seats to be occupied—in other words, so that the house may be full—and now they are overflowing; people anxious to use them are left standing outside. Though the fact be quite logical and natural, we cannot but recognise that this did not happen before and that now it does; consequently, there has been a change, an innovation, which justifies, at least for the first moment, our surprise.

To be surprised, to wonder, is to begin to understand. This is the sport, the luxury, special to the intellectual man. The gesture characteristic of his tribe consists in looking at the world with eyes wide open in wonder. Everything in the world is strange and marvellous to well-open eyes. This faculty of wonder is the delight refused to your football "fan," and, on the other hand, is the one which leads the intellectual man through life in the perpetual ecstasy of the visionary. His special at-tribute is the wonder of the eyes. Hence it was that the ancients gave Minerva her owl, the bird with ever-dazzled eyes.

Agglomeration, fullness, was not frequent before. Why

then is it now? The components of the multitudes around us have not sprung from nothing. Approximately the same number of people existed fifteen years ago. Indeed, after the war it might seem natural that their number should be less. Nevertheless, it is here we come up against the first important point. The individuals who made up these multitudes existed, but not *qua* multitude. Scattered about the world in small groups, or solitary, they lived a life, to all appearances, divergent, dissociate, apart. Each individual or small group occupied a place, its own, in country, village, town, or quarter of the great city. Now, suddenly, they appear as an agglomeration, and looking in any direction our eyes meet with the multitudes. Not only in any direction, but precisely in the best places, the relatively refined creation of human culture, previously reserved to lesser groups, in a word, to minorities. The multitude has suddenly become visible, installing itself in the preferential positions in society. Before, if it existed, it passed unnoticed, occupying the background of the social stage; now it has advanced to the footlights and is the principal character. There are no longer protagonists; there is only the chorus.

The concept of the multitude is quantitative and visual. Without changing its nature, let us translate it into terms of sociology. We then meet with the notion of the "social mass." Society is always a dynamic unity of two component factors: minorities and masses. The minorities are individuals or groups of individuals which are specially qualified. The mass is the assemblage of persons not specially qualified. By masses, then, is not to be understood, solely or mainly, "the working masses." The mass is the average man. In this way what was mere quantity— the multitude—is converted into a qualitative determination: it becomes the common social quality, man as undifferentiated from other men, but as repeating in himself

a generic type. What have we gained by this conversion
of quantity into quality? Simply this: by means of the
latter we understand the genesis of the former. It is evident to the verge of platitude that the normal formation
of a multitude implies the coincidence of desires, ideas,
ways of life, in the individuals who constitute it. It will
be objected that this is just what happens with every social
group, however select it may strive to be. This is true;
but there is an essential difference. In those groups which
are characterised by not being multitude and mass, the
effective coincidence of its members is based on some
desire, idea, or ideal, which of itself excludes the great
number. To form a minority, of whatever kind, it is necessary beforehand that each member separate himself from
the multitude for *special*, relatively personal, reasons.
Their coincidence with the others who form the minority
is, then, secondary, posterior to their having each adopted
an attitude of singularity, and is consequently, to a large
extent, a coincidence in not coinciding. There are cases
in which this singularising character of the group appears
in the light of day: those English groups, which style
themselves "nonconformists," where we have the group-
ing together of those who agree only in their disagree-
ment in regard to the limitless multitude. This coming together of the minority precisely in order to separate themselves from the majority is a necessary ingredient in the
formation of every minority. Speaking of the limited public which listened to a musician of refinement, Mallarmé
wittily says that this public by its presence in small numbers stressed the absence of the multitude.

Strictly speaking, the mass, as a psychological fact, can
be defined without waiting for individuals to appear in
mass formation. In the presence of one individual we can
decide whether he is "mass" or not. The mass is all that
which sets no value on itself—good or ill—based on spe-

cific grounds, but which feels itself "just like everybody," and nevertheless is not concerned about it; is, in fact, quite happy to feel itself as one with everybody else. Imagine a humble-minded man who, having tried to estimate his own worth on specific grounds—asking himself if he has any talent for this or that, if he excels in any direction— realises that he possesses no quality of excellence. Such a man will feel that he is mediocre and commonplace, ill-gifted, but will not feel himself "mass."

When one speaks of "select minorities" it is usual for the evil-minded to twist the sense of this expression, pretending to be unaware that the select man is not the petulant person who thinks himself superior to the rest, but the man who demands more of himself than the rest, even though he may not fulfil in his person those higher exigencies. For there is no doubt that the most radical division that it is possible to make of humanity is that which splits it into two classes of creatures: those who make great demands on themselves, piling up difficulties and duties; and those who demand nothing special of themselves, but for whom to live is to be every moment what they already are, without imposing on themselves any effort towards perfection; mere buoys that float on the waves. This reminds me that orthodox Buddhism is composed of two distinct religions: one, more rigorous and difficult, the other easier and more trivial: the Mahayana —"great vehicle" or "great path"—and the Hinayana— "lesser vehicle" or "lesser path." The decisive matter is whether we attach our life to one or the other vehicle, to a maximum or a minimum of demands upon ourselves.

The division of society into masses and select minorities is, then, not a division into social classes, but into classes of men, and cannot coincide with the hierarchic separation of "upper" and "lower" classes. It is, of course, plain that in these "upper" classes, when and as long as

they really are so, there is much more likelihood of finding men who adopt the "great vehicle," whereas the
"lower" classes normally comprise individuals of minus
quality. But, strictly speaking, within both these social
classes, there are to be found mass and genuine minority.
As we shall see, a characteristic of our times is the predominance, even in groups traditionally selective, of the
mass and the vulgar. Thus, in the intellectual life, which
of its essence requires and presupposes qualification, one
can note the progressive triumph of the pseudo-intellec-
tual, unqualified, unqualifiable, and, by their very mental
texture, disqualified. Similarly, in the surviving groups of
the "nobility," male and female. On the other hand, it is
not rare to find to-day amongst working men, who before
might be taken as the best example of what we are calling
"mass," nobly disciplined minds.

There exist, then, in society, operations, activities, and
functions of the most diverse order, which are of their
very nature special, and which consequently cannot be
properly carried out without special gifts. For example:
certain pleasures of an artistic and refined character, or
again the functions of government and of political judgment in public affairs. Previously these special activities
were exercised by qualified minorities, or at least by those
who claimed such qualification. The mass asserted no
right to intervene in them; they realised that if they
wished to intervene they would necessarily have to acquire those special qualities and cease being mere mass.
They recognised their place in a healthy dynamic social
system.

If we now revert to the facts indicated at the start,
they will appear clearly as the heralds of a changed
attitude in the mass. They all indicate that the mass has
decided to advance to the foreground of social life, to
occupy the places, to use the instruments and to enjoy

the pleasures hitherto reserved to the few. It is evident, for example, that the places were never intended for the multitude, for their dimensions are too limited, and the crowd is continuously overflowing; thus manifesting to our eyes and in the clearest manner the new phenomenon: the mass, without ceasing to be mass, is supplanting the minorities.

No one, I believe, will regret that people are to-day enjoying themselves in greater measure and numbers than before, since they have now both the desire and the means of satisfying it. The evil lies in the fact that this decision taken by the masses to assume the activities proper to the minorities is not, and cannot be, manifested solely in the domain of pleasure, but that it is a general feature of our time. Thus—to anticipate what we shall see later—I believe that the political innovations of recent times signify nothing less than the political domination of the masses. The old democracy was tempered by a generous dose of liberalism and of enthusiasm for law. By serving these principles the individual bound himself to maintain a severe discipline over himself. Under the shelter of liberal principles and the rule of law, minorities could live and act. Democracy and law—life in common under the law —were synonymous. To-day we are witnessing the triumphs of a hyperdemocracy in which the mass acts directly, outside the law, imposing its aspirations and its desires by means of material pressure. It is a false interpretation of the new situation to say that the mass has grown tired of politics and handed over the exercise of it to specialised persons. Quite the contrary. That was what happened previously; that was democracy. The mass took it for granted that after all, in spite of their defects and weaknesses, the minorities understood a little more of public problems than it did itself. Now, on the other hand, the mass believes that it has the right to impose and to give force of law to notions born in the café. I doubt whether there have been other periods of history in which the multitude has come to govern more directly than in our own. That is why I speak of hyperdemocracy.

The same thing is happening in other orders, particularly in the intellectual. I may be mistaken, but the present-day writer, when he takes his pen in hand to treat a subject which he has studied deeply, has to bear in mind that the average reader, who has never concerned himself with this subject, if he reads does so with the view, not of learning something from the writer, but rather, of pronouncing judgment on him when he is not in agreement with the commonplaces that the said reader carries in his head. If the individuals who make up the mass believed themselves specially qualified, it would be a case merely of personal error, not a sociological subversion. *The characteristic of the hour is that the commonplace mind, knowing itself to be commonplace, has the assurance to proclaim the rights of the commonplace and to impose them wherever it will.* As they say in the United States: "to be different is to be indecent." The mass crushes beneath it everything that is different, everything that is excellent, individual, qualified and select. Anybody who is not like everybody, who does not think like everybody, runs the risk of being eliminated. And it is clear, of course, that this "everybody" is not "everybody." "Everybody" was normally the complex unity of the mass and the divergent, specialised minorities. Nowadays, "everybody" is the mass alone. Here we have the formidable fact of our times, described without any concealment of the brutality of its features.

2

The Rise of the Historic Level

SUCH, then, is the formidable fact of our times, described without any concealment of the brutality of its features. It is, furthermore, entirely new in the history of our modern civilisation. Never, in the course of its development, has anything similar happened. If we wish to find its like we shall have to take a leap outside our modern history and immerse ourselves in a world, a vital element, entirely different from our own; we shall have to penetrate the ancient world till we reach the hour of its decline. The history of the Roman Empire is also the history of the uprising of the Empire of the Masses, who absorb and annul the directing minorities and put themselves in their place. Then, also, is produced the phenomenon of agglomeration, of "the full." For that reason, as Spengler has very well observed, it was necessary, just as in our day, to construct enormous buildings. The epoch of the masses is the epoch of the colossal.[1] We are living, then, under the brutal empire of the masses. Just so; I have now twice called this empire "brutal," and have thus paid my tribute to the god of the commonplace. Now, ticket in hand, I can cheerfully enter into my sub-

[1] The tragic thing about this process is that while these agglomerations were in formation there was beginning that depopulation of the countryside which was to result in an absolute decrease of the number of inhabitants in the Empire.

ject, see the show from inside. Or perhaps it was thought
that I was going to be satisfied with that description,
possibly exact, but quite external; the mere features, the
aspect under which this tremendous fact presents itself
when looked at from the view-point of the past? If I
were to leave the matter here and strangle off my present
essay without more ado, the reader would be left thinking, and quite justly, that this fabulous uprising of the
masses above the surface of history inspired me merely
with a few petulant, disdainful words, a certain amount
of hatred and a certain amount of disgust. This all the
more in my case, when it is well known that I uphold a
radically aristocratic interpretation of history. Radically,
because I have never said that human society *ought* to be
aristocratic, but a great deal more than that. What I have
said, and still believe with ever-increasing conviction, is
that human society *is* always, whether it will or no, aristocratic by its very essence, to the extreme that it is a
society in the measure that it is aristocratic, and ceases
to be such when it ceases to be aristocratic. Of course I
am speaking now of society and not of the State. No one
can imagine that, in the face of this fabulous seething of
the masses, it is the aristocratic attitude to be satisfied
with making a supercilious grimace, like a fine gentleman
of Versailles. Versailles—the Versailles of the grimaces—
does not represent aristocracy; quite the contrary, it is
the death and dissolution of a magnificent aristocracy.
For this reason, the only element of aristocracy left in
such beings was the dignified grace with which their
necks received the attentions of the guillotine; they accepted it as the tumour accepts the lancet. No; for anyone who has a sense of the real mission of aristocracies,
the spectacle of the mass incites and enflames him, as the
sight of virgin marble does the sculptor. Social aristocracy
has no resemblance whatever to that tiny group which

claims for itself alone the name of society, which calls itself "Society"; people who live by inviting or not inviting one another. Since everything in the world has its virtue and its mission, so within the vast world this small "smart world" has its own, but it is a very subordinate mission, not to be compared with the herculean task of genuine aristocracies. I should have no objection to discussing the meaning that lies in this smart world, to all appearance so meaningless, but our subject is now one of greater proportions. Of course, this self-same "distinguished society" goes with the times. Much food for thought was given me by a certain *jeune fille en fleur*, full of youth and modernity, a star of the first magnitude in the firmament of "smart" Madrid, when she said to me: "I can't stand a dance to which less than eight hundred people have been invited." Behind this phrase I perceived that the style of the masses is triumphant over the whole area of modern life, and imposes itself even in those sheltered corners which seemed reserved for the "happy few."

I reject equally, then, the interpretation of our times which does not lay clear the positive meaning hidden under the actual rule of the masses and that which accepts it blissfully, without a shudder of horror. Every destiny is dramatic, tragic in its deepest meaning. Whoever has not felt the danger of our times palpitating under his hand, has not really penetrated to the vitals of destiny, he has merely pricked its surface. The element of terror in the destiny of our time is furnished by the overwhelming and violent moral upheaval of the masses; imposing, invincible, and treacherous, as is destiny in every case. Whither is it leading us? Is it an absolute evil or a possible good? There it is, colossal, astride our times like a giant, a cosmic note of interrogation, always of uncertain shape, with something in it of the guillotine or the gallows, but also with something that strives to round itself into a triumphal arch.

The fact that we must submit to examination may be formulated under two headings: first, the masses are to-day exercising functions in social life which coincide with those which hitherto seemed reserved to minorities; and secondly, these masses have at the same time shown themselves indocile to the minorities—they do not obey them, follow them, or respect them; on the contrary, they push them aside and supplant them.

Let us analyse what comes under the first heading. By it I mean that the masses enjoy the pleasures and use the instruments invented by the select groups, and hitherto exclusively at the service of the latter. They feel appetites and needs which were previously looked upon as refinements, inasmuch as they were the patrimony of the few. Take a trivial example: in 1820 there cannot have been ten bathrooms in private houses in Paris (see the *Memoirs of the Comtesse de Boigne*). But furthermore, the masses to-day are acquainted with, and use with relative skill, many of the technical accomplishments previously confined to specialised individuals. And this refers not only to the technique of material objects, but, more important, to that of laws and society. In the XVIIIth Century, certain minority groups discovered that every human being, by the mere fact of birth, and without requiring any special qualification whatsoever, possessed certain fundamental political rights, the so-called rights of the man and the citizen; and further that, strictly speaking, these rights, common to all, are the only ones that exist.

Every other right attached to special gifts was condemned as being a privilege. This was at first a mere theory, the idea of a few men; then those few began to put the idea into practice, to impose it and insist upon it. Nevertheless, during the whole of the XIXth Century, the mass, while gradually becoming enthusiastic for those rights as an ideal, did not feel them as rights, did not exercise them or attempt to make them prevail, but, in fact, under democratic legislation, continued to feel itself just as under the old regime. The "people"—as it was then called—the "people" had learned that it was sovereign, but did not believe it. To-day the ideal has been changed into a reality; not only in legislation, which is the mere framework of public life, but in the heart of every individual, whatever his ideas may be, and even if he be a reactionary in his ideas, *that is to say, even when he attacks and castigates institutions by which those rights are sanctioned.* To my mind, anyone who does not realise this curious moral situation of the masses can understand nothing of what is to-day beginning to happen in the world. The sovereignty of the unqualified individual, of the human being as such, generically, has now passed from being a juridical idea or ideal to be a psychological state inherent in the average man. And note this, that when what was before an ideal becomes a component part of reality, it inevitably ceases to be an ideal. The prestige and the magic that are attributes of the ideal are volatilised. The levelling demands of a generous democratic inspiration have been changed from aspirations and ideals into appetites and unconscious assumptions.

Now, the meaning of this proclamation of the rights of man was none other than to lift human souls from their interior servitude and to implant within them a certain consciousness of mastery and dignity. Was it not this that it was hoped to do, namely, that the average man should feel himself master, lord, and ruler of himself and of his life? Well, that is now accomplished. Why, then, these complaints of the liberals, the democrats, the progressives of thirty years ago? Or is it that, like children, they want something, but not the consequences of that something? You want the ordinary man to be master. Well, do not be surprised if he acts for himself, if he demands all forms of enjoyment, if he firmly asserts his will, if he refuses all kinds of service, if he ceases to be docile to anyone, if he considers his own person and his own leisure, if he is careful as to dress: these are some of the attributes permanently attached to the consciousness of mastership. To-day we find them taking up their abode in the ordinary man, in the mass.

The situation, then, is this: the life of the ordinary man is to-day made up of the same "vital repertory" which before characterised only the superior minorities. Now the average man represents the field over which the history of each period acts; he is to history what sea-level is to geography. If, therefore, to-day the mean-level lies at a point previously only reached by aristocracies, the signification of this is simply that the level of history has suddenly risen—after long subterraneous preparations, it is true—but now quite plainly to the eyes, suddenly, at a bound, in one generation. Human life taken as a whole has mounted higher. The soldier of to-day, we might say, has a good deal of the officer; the human army is now made up of officers. Enough to watch the energy, the determination, the ease with which each individual moves through life to-day, snatches at the passing pleasure, imposes his personal will.

Everything that is good and bad in the present and in the immediate future has its cause and root in the general rise of the historic level. But here an observation that had not previously occurred to us presents itself. This fact, that the ordinary level of life to-day is that of the former minorities, is a new fact in Europe, but in America the natural, the "constitutional" fact. To realise my point, let the reader consider the matter of consciousness of equality before the law. That psychological state of feeling lord and master of oneself and equal to anybody else, which in Europe only outstanding groups succeeded in acquiring, was in America since the XVIIIth Century (and therefore, practically speaking, always) the natural state of things. And a further coincidence, still more curious, is this: when this psychological condition of the ordinary man appeared in Europe, when the level of his existence rose, the tone and manners of European life in all orders suddenly took on a new appearance which caused many people to say: "Europe is becoming Americanised." Those who spoke in this way gave no further attention to the matter; they thought it was a question of a slight change of custom, a fashion, and, deceived by the look of things, attributed it to some influence or other of America on Europe. This, to my mind, is simply to trivialise a question which is much more subtle and pregnant with surprises. Gallantry here makes an attempt to suborn me into telling our brothers beyond the sea that, in fact, Europe has become Americanised, and that this is due to an influence of America on Europe. But no; truth comes into conflict with gallantry, and it must prevail. Europe has not been Americanised; it has received no great influence from America. Possibly both these things are beginning to happen just now; but they did not occur in the recent part of which the present is the flowering. There is floating around a bewildering mass of false ideas which blind the vision of both parties, Americans and Europeans. The triumph of the masses and the consequent magnificent uprising of the vital level have come about in Europe for internal reasons, after two centuries of education of the multitude towards progress and a parallel economic improvement in society. But it so happens that the result coincides with the most marked aspect of American life; and on account of this coincidence of the moral situation of the ordinary man in Europe and in America, it has come about that for the first time the European understands American life which was to him before an enigma and a mystery. There is no question, then, of an influence, which indeed would be a little strange, would be, in fact, a "refluence," but of something which is still less suspected, namely, of a levelling. It has always been obscurely seen by Europeans that the general level of life in America was higher than in the Old World. It was the intuition, strongly felt, if unanalysed, of this fact which gave rise to the idea, always accepted, never challenged, that the future lies with America. It will be understood that such an idea, widespread and deep-rooted, did not float down on the wind, as it is said that orchids grow rootless in the air. The basis of it was the realisation of a higher level of average existence in America, in contrast with a lower level in the select minorities there as compared with those of Europe. But history, like agriculture, draws its nourishment from the valleys and not from the heights, from the average social level and not from men of eminence.

We are living in a levelling period; there is a levelling of fortunes, of culture among the various social classes, of the sexes. Well, in the same way there is a levelling of continents, and as the European was formerly lower from a vital point of view, he has come out the gainer from this levelling. Consequently, from this standpoint, the uprising of the masses implies a fabulous increase of vital possibilities, quite the contrary of what we hear so often about the decadence of Europe. This is a confused and clumsy expression, in which it is not clear what is being referred to, whether it is the European states, or European culture, or what lies underneath all this, and is of infinitely greater importance, the vital activity of Europe.

Of European states and culture we shall have a word

to say later on—though perhaps what we have already said is enough—but as regards the vitality, it is well to make clear from the start that we are in the presence of a gross error. Perhaps if I give it another turn, my statement may appear more convincing or less improbable; I say, then, that to-day the average Italian, Spaniard, or German is less differentiated in vital tone from the North American or the Argentine than he was thirty years ago. And this is a fact that the people of America ought not to forget.

3

The Height of the Times

THE rule of the masses, then, presents a favourable aspect, inasmuch as it signifies an all-round rise in the historical level, and reveals that average existence to-day moves on a higher altitude than that of yesterday. This brings home to us the fact that life can have different altitudes, and that there is a deep sense in the phrase that is often senselessly repeated when people speak of the height of our times. It will be well to pause and consider here, because this point offers us a means of establishing one of the most surprising characteristics of our age.

It is said, for example, that this or that matter is not worthy of the height of a certain time. And, in fact, not the abstract time of chronology, of the whole temporal plain, but the vital time, what each generation calls "our time," has always a certain elevation; is higher to-day than yesterday, or keeps on the level, or falls below it. The idea of falling contained in the word decadence has its origin in this intuition. Likewise, each individual feels, with more or less clearness, the relation which his own life bears to the height of the time through which he is passing. There are those who feel amid the manifestations of actual existence like a shipwrecked man who cannot keep his head above water. The *tempo* at which things move at present, the force and energy with which everything is done, cause anguish to the man of archaic mould, and this anguish is the measure of the difference between his pulse-beats and the pulse-beats of the time. On the other

28

hand, the man who lives completely and pleasurably in agreement with actual modes is conscious of the relation between the level of our time and that of various past times. What is this relation?

It would be wrong to suppose that the man of any particular period always looks upon past times as below the level of his own, simply because they are past. It is enough to recall that to the seeming of Jorge Manrique, "Any time gone by was better." But this is not the truth either. Not every age has left itself inferior to any past age, nor have all believed themselves superior to every preceding age. Every historical period displays a different feeling in respect of this strange phenomenon of the vital altitude, and I am surprised that thinkers and historians have never taken note of such an evident and important fact. Taken very roughly, the impression described by Jorge Manrique has certainly been the most general one. The majority of historical periods did not look upon their own time as superior to preceding ages. On the contrary, the most usual thing has been for men to dream of better times in a vague past, of a fuller existence; of a "golden age," as those taught by Greece and Rome have it; the Alcheringa of the Australian bushmen. This indicates that such men feel the pulse of their own lives lacking in full vigour, incapable of completely flooding their blood channels. For this reason they looked with respect on the past, on "classic" epochs, when existence seemed to them fuller, richer, more perfect and strenuous than the life of their own time. As they looked back and visualized those epochs of greater worth, they had the feeling, not of dominating them, but, on the contrary, of falling below them, just as a degree of temperature, if it possessed consciousness, might feel that it does not contain within itself the higher degree, that there are more calories in this than in itself. From A.D. 150 on, this impression of a shrinking of vitality, of a falling from position, of decay and loss of pulse shows itself increasingly in the Roman Empire. Had not Horace already sung: "Our fathers, viler than our grandfathers, begot us who are even viler, and we shall bring forth a progeny more degenerate still"? [1]

Two centuries later there were not in the whole Empire sufficient men of Italian birth with courage equal to filling the places of the centurions, and it was found necessary to hire for this post first Dalmatians, and afterwards Barbarians from the Danube and the Rhine. In the meantime the women were becoming barren, and Italy was depopulated.

Let us now turn to another kind of epoch which enjoys a vital sentiment, seemingly the most opposed to the last. We have here a very curious phenomenon which it is most important should be defined. When not more than thirty years ago politicians used to perorate before the crowds, it was their custom to condemn such and such a Government measure, some excess or other on its part, by saying that it was unworthy of the advanced times. It is curious to recall that we find the same phrase employed by Trajan in his famous letter to Pliny, advising him not to persecute the Christians on the strength of anonymous accusations: *nec nostri saeculi est*. There have been, then, various periods in history which have felt themselves as having attained a full, definitive height, periods in which it is thought that the end of a journey has been reached, a long-felt desire obtained, a hope completely fulfilled. This is "the plenitude of the time," the full ripening of historic life. And, in fact, thirty years

---

[1] Aetas parentum pejor avis tulit
nos nequiores, mox daturos
progeniem vitiosiorem.
                    Odes, III. 6.

ago, the European believed that human life had come to be what it ought to be, what for generations previous it had been desiring to be, what it was henceforward always bound to be. These epochs of plenitude always regard themselves as the result of many other preparatory periods, of other times lacking in plenitude, inferior to their own, above which this time of full-flower has risen. Seen from this height, those preparatory periods give the impression that during them life was an affair of mere longing and illusion unrealised, of unsatisfied desire, of eager precursors, a time of "not yet," of painful contrast between the definite aspiration and the reality which does not correspond to it. Thus the XIXth Century looks upon the Middle Ages. At length, the day arrives on which that old, sometimes agelong, desire seems to be fully attained, reality accepts it and submits to it. We have arrived at the heights we had in view, the goal to which we had looked forward, the summit of time. To "not yet" has succeeded "at last."

This was the feeling with regard to their own time held by our fathers and all their century. Let it not be forgotten; our time is a time which follows on a period of plenitude. Hence it is that, inevitably, the man living on the other bank, the man of that plenary epoch just past, who sees everything from his own view-point, will suffer from the optical illusion of regarding our age as a fall from plenitude, as a decadent period. But the lifelong student of history, the practised feeler of the pulse of times, cannot allow himself to be deceived by this system of optics based on imaginary periods of plenitude. As I have said, for such a "plenitude of time" to exist, it is necessary that a long-felt desire, dragging its anxious, eager way through centuries, is at last one day satisfied, and in fact these plenary periods are times which are self-satisfied; occasionally, as in the XIXth Century, more

than satisfied with themselves.[1] But we are now beginning to realise that these centuries, so self-satisfied, so perfectly rounded-off, are dead within. *Genuine vital integrity does not consist in satisfaction, in attainment, in
arrival.* As Cervantes said long since: "The road is always
better than the inn." When a period has satisfied its desires, its ideal, this means that it desires nothing more; that
the wells of desire have been dried up. That is to say, our
famous plenitude is in reality a coming to an end. There
are centuries which die of self-satisfaction through not
knowing how to renew their desires, just as the happy
drone dies after the nuptial flight.[2]

Hence we have the astonishing fact that these epochs
of so-called plenitude have always felt in the depths of
their consciousness a special form of sadness. The desires
so long in conception, which the XIXth Century seems
at last to realise, is what it named for itself in a word as
"modern culture." The very name is a disturbing one;
this time calls itself "modern," that is to say, final, definitive, in whose presence all the rest is mere preterite,
humble preparation and aspiration towards this present.
Nerveless arrows which miss their mark! [3]

[1] In the moulds for the coinage of Hadrian, we read phrases such
as these: *Italia Felix, Saeculum aureum, Tellus stabilita, Temporum
felicitas.* Besides the great work on numismatics of Cohen, see the
coins reproduced in Rostowzeff, *Social and Economic History of
the Roman Empire,* 1926, Plate LII, and p. 588, note 6.

[2] The wonderful pages of Hegel on periods of self-satisfaction in
his *Philosophy of History* should be read.

[3] The primary meaning of the words "modern," "modernity," with
which recent times have baptised themselves, brings out very
sharply that feeling of "the height of time" which I am at present
analysing. "Modern" is what is "in the fashion," that is to say, the
new fashion or modification which has arisen over against the old
traditional fashions used in the past. The word "modern" then ex-
presses a consciousness of a new life, superior to the old one, and
at the same time an imperative call to be at the height of one's
time. For the "modern" man, not to be "modern" means to fall
below the historic level.

Do we not here touch upon the essential difference between our time and that which has just passed away? Our time, in fact, no longer regards itself as definitive; on the contrary, it discovers, though obscurely, deep within itself an intuition that there are no such epochs, definitive, assured, crystallised for ever. Quite the reverse, the claim that a certain type of existence—the so-called "modern culture"—is definitive seems to us an incredible narrowing down and shutting out of the field of vision. And as an effect of this feeling we enjoy a delightful impression of having escaped from a hermetically sealed enclosure, of having regained freedom, of coming out once again under the stars into the world of reality, the world of the profound, the terrible, the unforeseeable, the inexhaustible, where everything is possible, the best and the worst. That faith in modern culture was a gloomy one. It meant that to-morrow was to be in all essentials similar to to-day, that progress consisted merely in advancing, for all time to be, along a road identical to the one already under our feet. Such a road is rather a kind of elastic prison which stretches on without ever setting us free. When in the early stages of the Empire some cultured provincial —Lucan or Seneca—arrived in Rome, and saw the magnificent imperial buildings, symbols of an enduring power, he felt his heart contract within him. Nothing new could now happen in the world. Rome was eternal. And if there is a melancholy of ruins which rises above them like exhalations from stagnant waters, this sensitive provincial felt a melancholy no less heavy, though of opposite sign: the melancholy of buildings meant for eternity.

Over against this emotional state, is it not clear that the feelings of our time are more like the noisy joy of children let loose from school? Nowadays we no longer know what is going to happen to-morrow in our world, and this causes us a secret joy; because that very impossibility of foresight, that horizon ever open to all contingencies, constitute authentic life, the true fullness of our existence. This diagnosis, the other aspect of which, it is true, is lacking, stands in contrast to the plaints of decadence which wail forth in the pages of so many contemporary writers. We are in the presence of an optical illusion arising from a multiplicity of causes. I shall consider certain of these some other time; for the moment I wish to advance the most obvious one. It arises from the fact that, faithful to an ideology which I consider a thing of the past, only the political or cultural aspects of history are considered, and it is not realised that these are the mere surface of history; that in preference to, and deeper than, these, the reality of history lies in biological power, in pure vitality, in what there is in man of cosmic energy, not identical with, but related to, the energy which agitates the sea, fecundates the beast, causes the tree to flower and the star to shine.

As an offset to the diagnosis of pessimism, I recommend the following consideration. Decadence is, of course, a comparative concept. Decline is from a higher to a lower state. But this comparison may be made from the most varied points of view imaginable. To the manufacturer of amber mouthpieces this is a decadent world, for nowadays hardly anyone smokes from amber mouthpieces. Other view-points may be more dignified than this one, but strictly speaking none of them escapes being partial, arbitrary, external to that very life whose constituents we are attempting to assay. There is only one view-point which is justifiable and natural; to take up one's position in life itself, to look at it from the inside, and to see if it feels itself decadent, that is to say, diminished, weakened, insipid. But even when we look at it from the inside, how can we know whether life feels itself on the decline or not? To my mind there can be no doubt as to the

decisive symptom: a life which does not give the preference to any other life, of any previous period, which
therefore prefers its own existence, cannot in any serious sense be called decadent. This is the point towards
which all my discussion of the problem of the height of
times was leading, and it turns out that it is precisely our
time which in this matter enjoys a most strange sensation,
unique, as far as I know, in recorded history.

In the drawing-room gatherings of last century there
inevitably arrived a moment when the ladies and their
tame poets put this question, one to the other: "At what
period of history would you like to have lived?" And
straightaway each of them, making a bundle of his own
personal existence, started off on an imaginary tramp
along the roads of history in search of a period into
which that existence might most delightfully fit. And the
reason was that, although feeling itself, because it felt
itself, arrived at plenitude, the XIXth Century was still,
in actual fact, bound to the past, on whose shoulders it
thought it was standing; it saw itself actually as the cul-
mination of that past. Hence it still believed in periods
relatively classic—the age of Pericles, the Renaissance—
during which the values that hold to-day were prepared.
This should be enough to cause suspicion of these periods
of plenitude; they have their faces turned backwards,
their eyes are on the past which they consider fulfilled
in themselves.

And now, what would be the sincere reply of any representative man of to-day if such a question were put
to him? I think there can be no doubt about it; any past
time, without exception, would give him the feeling of
a restricted space in which he could not breathe. That
is to say, the man of to-day feels that his life is more a life
than any past one, or, to put it the other way about, the
entirety of past time seems small to actual humanity. This

intuition as regards present-day existence renders null
by its stark clarity any consideration about decadence
that is not very cautiously thought out. To start with,
our present life feels itself as ampler than all previous lives.
How can it regard itself as decadent? Quite the contrary;
what has happened is, that through sheer regard of itself
as "more" life, it has lost all respect, all consideration for
the past. Hence for the first time we meet with a period
which makes *tabula rasa* of all classicism, which recognises in nothing that is past any possible model or standard,
and appearing as it does after so many centuries without
any break in evolution, yet gives the impression of a commencement, a dawn, an initiation, an infancy. We look
backwards and the famous Renaissance reveals itself as a
period of narrow provincialism, of futile gestures—why
not say the word?—*ordinary*.

Some time ago I summed up the situation in the following way: "This grave dissociation of past and present
is the generic fact of our time and the cause of the suspicion, more or less vague, which gives rise to the confusion characteristic of our present-day existence. We
feel that we actual men have suddenly been left alone on
the earth; that the dead did not die in appearance only
but effectively; that they can no longer help us. Any remains of the traditional spirit have evaporated. Models,
norms, standards are no use to us. We have to solve our
problems without any active collaboration of the past,
in full actuality, be they problems of art, science, or politics. The European stands alone, without any living ghosts
by his side; like Peter Schlehmil he has lost his shadow.
This is what always happens when midday comes." [1]

What, then, in a word is the "height of our times"?
It is not the fullness of time, and yet it feels itself superior
to all times past, and beyond all known fullness. It is not

[1] *The Dehumanisation of Art.*

easy to formulate the impression that our epoch has of itself; it believes itself more than all the rest, and at the same time feels that it is a beginning. What expression shall we find for it? Perhaps this one: superior to other times, inferior to itself. Strong, indeed, and at the same time uncertain of its destiny; proud of its strength and at the same time fearing it.

4

The Increase of Life

THE rule of the masses and the raising of the level, the height of the time which this indicates, are in their turn only symptoms of a more complete and more general fact. This fact is almost grotesque and incredible in its stark and simple truth. It is just this, that the world has suddenly grown larger, and with it and in it, life itself. To start with, life has become, in actual fact, world-wide in character; I mean that the content of existence for the average man of to-day includes the whole planet; that each individual habitually lives the life of the whole world. Something more than a year ago the people of Seville could follow, hour by hour, in the newspapers, what was happening to a few men near the North Pole; that is to say, that icebergs passed drifting against the burning back-ground of the Andalusian landscape. Each portion of the earth is no longer shut up in its own geometrical posi-tion, but for many of the purposes of human life acts upon other portions of the planet. In accordance with the physical principle that things are wherever their ef-fects are felt, we can attribute to-day to any point on the globe the most effective ubiquity. This nearness of the far-off, this presence of the absent, has extended in fabu-lous proportions the horizon of each individual existence.

And the world has also increased from the view-point of time. Prehistory and archaeology have discovered his-torical periods of fantastic duration. Whole civilisations and empires of which till recently not even the name was suspected, have been annexed to our knowledge like new continents. The illustrated paper and the film have brought these far-off portions of the universe before the immediate vision of the crowd.

But this spatio-temporal increase of the world would of itself signify nothing. Physical space and time are the absolutely stupid aspects of the universe. Hence, there is more reason than is generally allowed in that worship of mere speed which is at present being indulged in by our contemporaries. Speed, which is made up of space and time, is no less stupid than its constituents, but it serves to nullify them. One stupidity can only be overcome by another. It was a question of honour for man to triumph over cosmic space and time,[1] which are entirely devoid of meaning, and there is no reason for surprise at the fact that we get a childish pleasure out of the indulgence in mere speed, by means of which we kill space and strangle time. By annulling them, we give them life, we make them serve vital purposes, we can *be* in more places than we could before, enjoy more comings and goings, consume more cosmic time in less vital time.

But after all, the really important increase of our world does not lie in its greater dimensions, but in its containing many more things. Each of these things—the word is to be taken in its widest acceptation—is something which we can desire, attempt, do, undo, meet with, enjoy or repel; all notions which imply vital activities. Take any one of our ordinary activities; buying, for example. Imagine two men, one of the present day and one of the XVIIIth Century, possessed of equal fortunes relative to money-values in their respective periods, and compare

---

[1] It is precisely because man's vital time is limited, precisely because he is mortal, that he needs to triumph over distance and delay. For an immortal being, the motor-car would have no meaning.

the stock of purchasable things offered to each. The difference is almost fabulous. The range of possibilities opened out before the present-day purchaser has become practically limitless. It is not easy to think of and wish for anything which is not to be found in the market, and vice versa, it is not possible for a man to think of and wish for everything that is actually offered for sale. I shall be told that with a fortune relatively equal, the man of to-day cannot buy more goods than the man of the XVIIIth Century. This is not the case. Many more things can be bought to-day, because manufacture has cheapened all articles. But after all, even if it were the case, it would not concern my point, rather would it stress what I am trying to say. The purchasing activity ends in the decision to buy a certain object, but for that very reason it is previously an act of choice, and the choice begins by putting before oneself the possibilities offered by the market. Hence it follows that life, in its "purchasing" aspect, consists primarily in living over the possibilities of buying as such. When people talk of life they generally forget something which to me seems most essential, namely, that our existence is at every instant and primarily the consciousness of what is possible to us. If at every moment we had before us no more than one possibility, it would be meaningless to give it that name. Rather would it be a pure necessity. But there it is: this strangest of facts that a fundamental condition of our existence is that it always has before it various prospects, which by their variety acquire the character of possibilities among which we have to make our choice.[1] To say that we live is the same as saying that we find ourselves

[1] In the worst case, if the world seemed reduced to one single outlet there would still be two: either that or to leave the world. But leaving the world forms part of the world, as a door is part of a room.

in an atmosphere of definite possibilities. This atmosphere we generally call our "circumstances." All life means finding oneself in "circumstances" or in the world around us.[1] For this is the fundamental meaning of the idea "world." The world is the sum-total of our vital possibilities. It is not then something apart from and foreign to our existence, it is its actual periphery. It represents what it is within our power to be, our vital potentiality. This must be reduced to the concrete in order to be realised, or putting it another way, we become only a part of what it is possible for us to be. Hence it is that the world seems to us something enormous, and ourselves a tiny object within it. The world or our possible existence is always greater than our destiny or actual existence. But what I wanted to make clear just now was the extent to which the life of man has increased in the dimension of potentiality. It can now count on a range of possibilities fabulously greater than ever before. In the intellectual order it now finds more "paths of ideation," more problems, more data, more sciences, more points of view. Whereas the number of occupations in primitive life can almost be counted on the fingers of one hand—shepherd, hunter, warrior, seer—the list of possible avocations to-day is immeasurably long. Something similar occurs in the matter of pleasures, although (and this is a phenomenon of more importance than it seems) the catalogue of pleasures is not so overflowing as in other aspects of life. Nevertheless, for the man of the middle classes who lives in towns —and towns are representative of modern existence—the possibilities of enjoyment have increased, in the course of the present century, in fantastic proportion. But the

[1] See the prologue to my first book, *Meditaciones del Quijote*, 1916. In *Las Atlántidas* I use the word "horizon." See also the essay *El origen deportivo del Estado*, 1926, now included in Vol. 7 of *El Espectador*.

increase of vital potentiality is not limited to what we have said up to this. It has also grown in a more immediate and mysterious direction. It is a constant and well-known fact that in physical effort connected with sport, performances are "put up" to-day which excel to an extraordinary degree those known in the past. It is not enongh to wonder at each one in particular and to note that it beats the record, we must note the impression that their frequency leaves on the mind, convincing us that the human organism possesses in our days capacities superior to any it has previously had. For something similar happens in the case of science. In no more than a decade science has extended the cosmic horizon to an incredible degree. The physics of Einstein moves through spaces so vast, that the old physics of Newton seems by comparison lodged in an attic.[1] And this extensive increase is due to an intensive increase in scientific precision. Einstein's physics arose through attention to minute differences which previously were despised and disregarded as seeming of no importance. The atom, yesterday the final limit of the world, turns out to-day to have swollen to such an extent that it becomes a planetary system. In speaking of all this I am not referring to its importance in the perfecting of culture—that does not interest me for the moment—but as regards the increase of subjective potency which it implies. I am not stressing the fact that the physics of Einstein is more exact than the physics of Newton, but that the man Einstein is capable of greater exactitude and liberty of spirit [2] than the man Newton; just as the box-

[1] The world of Newton was infinite; but this infinity was not a matter of size, but an empty generalisation, an abstract, inane Utopia. The world of Einstein is finite, but full and concrete in all its parts, consequently a world richer in things and effectively of greater extent.

[2] Liberty of spirit, that is to say, intellectual power, is measured by its capacity to dissociate ideas traditionally inseparable. It costs

ing champion of to-day can give blows of greater "punch" than have ever been given before. Just as the cinematograph and the illustrated journals place before the eyes of the average man the remotest spots on the planet; newspapers and conversations supply him with accounts of these new intellectual feats, which are confirmed by the recently-invented technical apparatus which he sees in the shop windows. All this fills his mind with an impression of fabulous potentiality. By what I have said I do not mean to imply that human life is to-day better than at other times. I have not spoken of the quality of actual existence, but of its quantitative advance, its increase of potency. I believe I am thus giving an exact description of the conscience of the man of to-day, his vital tone, which consists in his feeling himself possessed of greater potentiality than ever before and in all previous time seeming dwarfed by the contrast. This description was necessary in order to meet the pronouncements on decadence, and specifically on the decadence of the West, which have filled the air in the last decade. Recall the argument with which I set out, and which appears to me as simple as it is obvious. It is useless to talk of decadence without making clear what is undergoing decay. Does this pessimistic term refer to culture? Is there a decadence of European culture? Or is there rather only a decadence of the national organisations of Europe? Let us take this to be the case. Would that entitle us to speak of Western decadence? By no means, for such forms of decadence are partial decreases relating to secondary historical elements—culture and nationality. There is only one absolute decadence; it consists in a lowering of vitality, and

---

more to dissociate ideas than to associate them, as Köhler has shown in his investigations on the intelligence of chimpanzees. Human understanding has never had greater power of dissociation than at present.

that only exists when it is felt as such. It is for this reason that I have delayed over the consideration of a phenomenon generally overlooked: the consciousness or sensation that every period has experienced of its own vital level. This led us to speak of the "plenitude" which some centuries have felt in regard to others which, conversely, looked upon themselves as having fallen from greater heights, from some far-off brilliant golden age. And I ended by noting the very plain fact that our age is characterised by the strange presumption that it is superior to all past time; more than that, by its leaving out of consideration all that is past, by recognising no classical or normative epochs, by looking on itself as a new life superior to all previous forms and irreducible to them. I doubt if our age can be understood without keeping firm hold on this observation, for that is precisely its special problem. If it felt that it was decadent, it would look on other ages as superior to itself, which would be equivalent to esteeming and admiring them and venerating the principles by which they were inspired. Our age would then have clear and firmly held ideals, even if incapable of realising them. But the truth is exactly the contrary; we live at a time when man believes himself fabulously capable of creation, but he does not know what to create. Lord of all things, he is not lord of himself. He feels lost amid his own abundance. With more means at its disposal, more knowledge, more technique than ever, it turns out that the world to-day goes the same way as the worst of worlds that have been; it simply drifts.

Hence the strange combination of a sense of power and a sense of insecurity which has taken up its abode in the soul of modern man. To him is happening what was said of the Regent during the minority of Louis XV: he had all the talents except the talent to make use of them. To the XIXth Century many things seemed no longer possible, firm-fixed as was its faith in progress. To-day, by the very fact that everything seems possible to us, we have a feeling that the worst of all is possible: retrogression, barbarism, decadence.[1] This of itself would not be a bad symptom; it would mean that we are once again forming contact with that insecurity which is essential to all forms of life, that anxiety both dolorous and delicious contained in every moment, if we know how to live it to its innermost core, right down to its palpitating vitals. Generally we refuse to feel that fearsome pulsation which makes of a moment of sincerity a tiny fleeting heart; we strain in the attempt to find security and to render ourselves insensible to the fundamental drama of our destiny, by steeping it in habits, usages, topics—in every kind of chloroform. It is an excellent thing, then, that for the first time for nearly three centuries we are surprised to find ourselves with the feeling that we do not know what is going to happen to-morrow.

Every man who adopts a serious attitude before his own existence and makes himself fully responsible for it will feel a certain kind of insecurity which urges him to keep ever on the alert. The gesture which the Roman Army Orders imposed on the sentinel of the Legion was that he should keep his finger on his lips to avoid drowsiness and to maintain his alertness. The gesture has its value, it seems to ordain an even greater silence during the silence of the night, so as to be able to catch the sound of the secret germination of the future. The security of periods of "plenitude"—such as the last century—is an optical illusion which leads to neglect of the future, all direction of which is handed over to the mechanism of the universe. Both progressive Liberalism and Marxist

[1] This is the root-origin of all our diagnoses of decadence. Not that we are decadent, but that, being predisposed to admit every possibility, we do not exclude that of decadence.

Socialism presume that what is desired by them as the best of possible futures will be necessarily realised, with necessity similar to that of astronomy. With consciences lulled by this idea, they have cast away the rudder of history, have ceased to keep their watch, have lost their agility and their efficiency. And so, life has escaped from their grasp, has become completely unsubmissive and to-day is floating around without any fixed course. Under his mask of generous futurism, the progressive no longer concerns himself with the future; convinced that it holds in store for him neither surprises nor secrets, nothing adventurous, nothing essentially new; assured that the world will now proceed on a straight course, neither turning aside nor dropping back, he puts away from him all anxiety about the future and takes his stand in the definite present. Can we be surprised that the world to-day seems empty of purposes, anticipations, ideals? Nobody has concerned himself with supplying them. Such has been the desertion of the directing minorities, which is always found on the reverse side of the rebellion of the masses.

But it is time for us to return to the consideration of this last. After having stressed the favourable aspect presented by the triumph of the masses, it will be well to descend now by the other slope, a much more dangerous one.

5

A Statistical Fact

This essay is an attempt to discover the diagnosis of our time, of our actual existence. We have indicated the first part of it, which may be resumed thus: our life as a programme of possibilities is magnificent, exuberant, superior to all others known to history. But by the very fact that its scope is greater, it has overflowed all the channels, principles, norms, ideals handed down by tradition. It is more life than all previous existence, and therefore all the more problematical. It can find no direction from the past.[1] It has to discover its own destiny.

But now we must complete the diagnosis. Life, which means primarily what is possible for us to be, is likewise, and for that very reason, a choice, from among these possibilities, of what we actually are going to be. Our circumstances—these possibilities—form the portion of life given us, imposed on us. This constitutes what we call the world. Life does not choose its own world, it finds itself, to start with, in a world determined and unchangeable: the world of the present. Our world is that portion of destiny which goes to make up our life. But this vital destiny is not a kind of mechanism. We are not launched into existence like a shot from a gun, with its trajectory absolutely predetermined. The destiny under

[1] We shall see, nevertheless, how it is possible to obtain from the past, if not positive orientation, certain negative counsel. The past will not tell us what we ought to do, but it will what we ought to avoid.

which we fall when we come into this world—it is always *this* world, the actual one—consists in the exact contrary. Instead of imposing on us one trajectory, it imposes several, and consequently forces us to choose. Surprising condition, this, of our existence! To live is to feel ourselves *fatally* obliged to exercise our *liberty*, to decide what we are going to be in this world. Not for a single moment is our activity of decision allowed to rest. Even when in desperation we abandon ourselves to whatever may happen, we have decided not to decide.

It is, then, false to say that in life "circumstances decide." On the contrary, circumstances are the dilemma, constantly renewed, in presence of which we have to make our decision; what actually decides is our character. All this is equally valid for collective life. In it also there is, first, a horizon of possibilities, and then, a determination which chooses and decides on the effective form of collective existence. This determination has its origin in the character of society, or what comes to the same thing, of the type of men dominant in it. In our time it is the mass-man who dominates, it is he who decides. It will not do to say that this is what happened in the period of democracy, of universal suffrage. Under universal suffrage, the masses do not decide, their role consists in supporting the decision of one minority or other. It was these who presented their "programmes"—excellent word. Such programmes were, in fact, programmes of collective life. In them the masses were invited to accept a line of decision.

To-day something very different is happening. If we observe the public life of the countries where the triumph of the masses has made most advance—these are the Mediterranean countries—we are surprised to find that politically they are living from day to day. The phenomenon is an extraordinarily strange one. Public author-

ity is in the hands of a representative of the masses. These
are so powerful that they have wiped out all opposition.
They are in possession of power in such an unassailable
manner that it would be difficult to find in history examples of a Government so all-powerful as these are. And
yet public authority—the Government—exists from hand
to mouth, it does not offer itself as a frank solution for
the future, it represents no clear announcement of the
future, it does not stand out as the beginning of something whose development or evolution is conceivable. In
short, it lives without any vital programme, any plan of
existence. It does not know where it is going, because,
strictly speaking, it has no fixed road, no predetermined
trajectory before it. When such a public authority attempts to justify itself it makes no reference at all to the
future. On the contrary, it shuts itself up in the present,
and says with perfect sincerity: "I am an abnormal form
of Government imposed by circumstances." Hence its
activities are reduced to dodging the difficulties of the
hour; not solving them, but escaping from them for the
time being, employing any methods whatsoever, even at
the cost of accumulating thereby still greater difficulties
for the hour which follows. Such has public power always been when exercised directly by the masses: omnipotent and ephemeral. The mass-man is he whose life
lacks any purpose, and simply goes drifting along. Consequently, though his possibilities and his powers be enormous, he constructs nothing. And it is this type of man
who decides in our time. It will be well, then, that we
analyse his character.

The key to this analysis is found when, returning to the
starting-point of this essay, we ask ourselves: "Whence
have come all these multitudes which nowadays fill to
overflowing the stage of history?" Some years ago the
eminent economist, Werner Sombart, laid stress on a very

simple fact, which I am surprised is not present to every mind which meditates on contemporary events. This very simple fact is sufficient of itself to clarify our vision of the Europe of to-day, or if not sufficient, puts us on the road to enlightenment. The fact is this: from the time European history begins in the VIth Century up to the year 1800—that is, through the course of twelve centuries —Europe does not succeed in reaching a total population greater than 180 million inhabitants. Now, from 1800 to 1914—little more than a century—the population of Europe mounts from 180 to 460 millions! I take it that the contrast between these figures leaves no doubt as to the prolific qualities of the last century. In three generations it produces a gigantic mass of humanity which, launched like a torrent over the historic area, has inundated it. This fact, I repeat, should suffice to make us realise the triumph of the masses and all that is implied and announced by it. Furthermore, it should be added as the most concrete item to that rising of the level of existence which I have already indicated.

But at the same time this fact proves to us how unfounded is our admiration when we lay stress on the increase of new countries like the United States of America. We are astonished at this increase, which has reached to 100 millions in a century, when the really astonishing fact is the teeming fertility of Europe. Here we have another reason for correcting the deceptive notion of the Americanisation of Europe. Not even that characteristic which might seem specifically American—the rapidity of increase in population—is peculiarly such. Europe has increased in the last century much more than America. America has been formed from the overflow of Europe.

But although this fact ascertained by Werner Sombart is not as well known as it should be, the confused idea of a considerable population increase in Europe was widespread enough to render unnecessary insistence on it. In the figures cited, then, it is not the increase of population which interests me, but the fact that by the contrast with the previous figures the dizzy rapidity of the increase is brought into relief. This is the point of importance for us at the moment. For that rapidity means that heap after heap of human beings have been dumped on to the historic scene at such an accelerated rate, that it has been difficult to saturate them with traditional culture. And in fact, the average type of European at present possesses a soul, healthier and stronger it is true than those of the last century, but much more simple. Hence, at times he leaves the impression of a primitive man suddenly risen in the midst of a very old civilisation. In the schools, which were such a source of pride to the last century, it has been impossible to do more than instruct the masses in the technique of modern life; it has been found impossible to educate them. They have been given tools for an intenser form of existence, but no feeling for their great historic duties; they have been hurriedly inoculated with the pride and power of modern instruments, but not with their spirit. Hence they will have nothing to do with their spirit, and the new generations are getting ready to take over command of the world as if the world were a paradise without trace of former footsteps, without traditional and highly complex problems.

To the last century, then, falls the glory and the responsibility of having let loose upon the area of history the great multitudes. And this fact affords the most suitable view-point in order to judge that century with equity. There must have been something extraordinary, incomparable, in it when such harvests of human fruit were produced in its climate. Any preference for the principles which inspired other past ages is frivolous and ridiculous if one does not previously show proof of having realised this magnificent fact and attempted to digest it. The whole of history stands out as a gigantic laboratory in which all possible experiments have been made to obtain a formula of public life most favourable to the plant "man." And beyond all possible explaining away, we find ourselves face to face with the fact that, by submitting the seed of humanity to the treatment of two principles, liberal democracy and technical knowledge, in a single century the species in Europe has been triplicated.

Such an overwhelming fact forces us, unless we prefer not to use our reason, to draw these conclusions: first, that liberal democracy based on technical knowledge is the highest type of public life hitherto known; secondly, that that type may not be the best imaginable, but the one we imagine as superior to it must preserve the essence of those two principles; and thirdly, that to return to any forms of existence inferior to that of the XIXth Century is suicidal.

Once we recognise this with all the clearness that the clearness of the fact itself demands we must then rise up against the XIXth Century. If it is evident that there was in it something extraordinary and incomparable, it is no less so that it must have suffered from certain radical vices, certain constitutional defects, when it brought into being a caste of men—the mass-man in revolt—who are placing in imminent danger those very principles to which they owe their existence. If that human type continues to be master in Europe, thirty years will suffice to send our continent back to barbarism. Legislative and industrial technique will disappear with the same facility with which so many trade secrets have often disappeared.[1] The whole

[1] Hermann Weyl, one of the greatest of present-day physicists, the companion and continuer of the work of Einstein, is in the habit of saying in conversation that if ten or twelve specified individuals were to die suddenly, it is almost certain that the marvels of physics to-day would be lost for ever to humanity. A preparation of many

of life will be contracted. The actual abundance of possibilities will change into practical scarcity, a pitiful impotence, a real decadence. For the rebellion of the masses is one and the same thing with what Rathenau called "the vertical invasion of the barbarians." It is of great importance, then, to understand thoroughly this mass-man with his potentialities of the greatest good and the greatest evil.

---

centuries has been needed in order to accommodate the mental organ to the abstract complexity of physical theory. Any event might annihilate such prodigious human possibilities, which in addition are the basis of future technical development.

6

The Dissection of the Mass-Man Begins

WHAT is he like, this mass-man who to-day dominates public life, political and non-political, and why is he like it, that is, how has he been produced?

It will be well to answer both questions together, for they throw light on one another. The man who to-day is attempting to take the lead in European existence is very different from the man who directed the XIXth Century, but he was produced and prepared by the XIXth Century. Any keen mind of the years 1820, 1850, and 1880 could by simple *a priori* reasoning, foresee the gravity of the present historical situation, and in fact nothing is happening now which was not foreseen a hundred years ago. "The masses are advancing," said Hegel in apocalyptic fashion. "Without some new spiritual influence, our age, which is a revolutionary age, will produce a catastrophe," was the pronouncement of Comte. "I see the flood-tide of nihilism rising," shrieked Nietzsche from a crag of the Engadine. It is false to say that history cannot be foretold. Numberless times this has been done. If the future offered no opening to prophecy, it could not be understood when fulfilled in the present and on the point of falling back into the past. The idea that the historian is on the reverse side a prophet, sums up the whole philosophy of history. It is true that it is only possible to anticipate the general structure of the future, but that is all that we in truth understand of the past or of the present. Accordingly, if you want a good view of your own age, look at it from far off. From what distance? The answer is simple. Just far enough to prevent you seeing Cleopatra's nose.

What appearance did life present to that multitudinous man who in ever-increasing abundance the XIXth Century kept producing? To start with, an appearance of universal material ease. Never had the average man been able to solve his economic problem with greater facility. Whilst there was a proportionate decrease of great fortunes and life became harder for the individual worker, the middle classes found their economic horizon widened every day. Every day added a new luxury to their standard of life. Every day their position was more secure and more independent of another's will. What before would have been considered one of fortune's gifts, inspiring humble gratitude towards destiny, was converted into a right, not to be grateful for, but to be insisted on.

From 1900 on, the worker likewise begins to extend and assure his existence. Nevertheless, he has to struggle to obtain his end. He does not, like the middle class, find the benefit attentively served up to him by a society and a state which are a marvel of organisation. To this ease and security of economic conditions are to be added the physical ones, comfort and public order. Life runs on smooth rails, and there is no likelihood of anything violent or dangerous breaking in on it. Such a free, untrammelled situation was bound to instil into the depths of such souls an idea of existence which might be expressed in the witty and penetrating phrase of an old country like ours: "Wide is Castile." That is to say, in all its primary and decisive aspects, life presented itself to the new man as *exempt from restrictions*. The realisation of this fact and of its importance becomes immediate when we remember

that such a freedom of existence was entirely lacking to
the common men of the past. On the contrary, for them
life was a burdensome destiny, economically and physically. From birth, existence meant to them an accumulation of impediments which they were obliged to suffer,
without possible solution other than to adapt themselves
to them, to settle down in the narrow space they left
available.

But still more evident is the contrast of situations, if
we pass from the material to the civil and moral. The
average man, from the second half of the XIXth Century
on, finds no social barriers raised against him. That is to
say, that as regards the forms of public life he no longer
finds himself from birth confronted with obstacles and
limitations. There is nothing to force him to limit his
existence. Here again, "Wide is Castile." There are no
"estates" or "castes." There are no civil privileges. The
ordinary man learns that all men are equal before the law.

Never in the course of history had man been placed
in vital surroundings even remotely familiar to those set
up by the conditions just mentioned. We are, in fact,
confronted with a radical innovation in human destiny,
implanted by the XIXth Century. A new stage has been
mounted for human existence, new both in the physical
and the social aspects. Three principles have made possible this new world: liberal democracy, scientific experiment, and industrialism. The two latter may be
summed up in one word: technicism. Not one of those
principles was invented by the XIXth Century; they
proceed from the two previous centuries. The glory of
the XIXth Century lies not in their discovery, but in their
implantation. No one but recognises that fact. But it is
not sufficient to recognise it in the abstract, it is necessary
to realise its inevitable consequences.

The XIXth Century was of its essence revolutionary.

This aspect is not to be looked for in the scenes of the barricades, which are mere incidents, but in the fact that it placed the average man—the great social mass—in conditions of life radically opposed to those by which he had always been surrounded. It turned his public existence upside down. Revolution is not the uprising against pre-existing order, but the setting up of a new order contradictory to the traditional one. Hence there is no exaggeration in saying that the man who is the product of the XIXth Century is, for the effects of public life, a man apart from all other men. The XVIIIth-Century man differs, of course, from the XVIIth-Century man, and this one in turn from his fellow of the XVIth Century, but they are all related, similar, even identical in essentials when confronted with this new man. For the "common" man of all periods "life" had principally meant limitation, obligation, dependence; in a word, pressure. Say oppression, if you like, provided it be understood not only in the juridical and social sense, but also in the cosmic. For it is this latter which has never been lacking up to a hundred years ago, the date at which starts the practically limitless expansion of scientific technique—physical and administrative. Previously, even for the rich and powerful, the world was a place of poverty, difficulty and danger.[1]

The world which surrounds the new man from his birth does not compel him to limit himself in any fashion, it sets up no veto in opposition to him; on the contrary,

[1] However rich an individual might be in relation to his fellows, as the world in its totality was poor, the sphere of conveniences and commodities with which his wealth furnished him was very limited. The life of the average man to-day is easier, more convenient and safer than that of the most powerful of another age. What difference does it make to him not to be richer than others if the world is richer and furnishes him with magnificent roads, railways, telegraphs, hotels, personal safety and aspirin?

it incites his appetite, which in principle can increase indefinitely. Now it turns out—and this is most important —that this world of the XIXth and early XXth Centuries not only has the perfections and the completeness which it actually possesses, but furthermore suggests to those who dwell in it the radical assurance that to-morrow it will be still richer, ampler, more perfect, as if it enjoyed a spontaneous, inexhaustible power of increase. Even to-day, in spite of some signs which are making a tiny breach in that sturdy faith, even to-day, there are few men who doubt that motorcars will in five years' time be more comfortable and cheaper than to-day. They believe in this as they believe that the sun will rise in the morning. The metaphor is an exact one. For, in fact, the common man, finding himself in a world so excellent, technically and socially, believes that it has been produced by nature, and never thinks of the personal efforts of highly-endowed individuals which the creation of this new world presupposed. Still less will he admit the notion that all these facilities still require the support of certain difficult human virtues, the least failure of which would cause the rapid disappearance of the whole magnificent edifice.

This leads us to note down in our psychological chart of the mass-man of to-day two fundamental traits: the free expansion of his vital desires, and therefore, of his personality; and his radical ingratitude towards all that has made possible the ease of his existence. These traits together make up the well-known psychology of the spoilt child. And in fact it would entail no error to use this psychology as a "sight" through which to observe the soul of the masses of to-day. Heir to an ample and generous past—generous both in ideals and in activities —the new commonalty has been spoiled by the world around it. To spoil means to put no limit on caprice, to give one the impression that everything is permitted to

him and that he has no obligations. The young child
exposed to this regime has no experience of its own limits. By reason of the removal of all external restraint, all
clashing with other things, he comes actually to believe
that he is the only one that exists, and gets used to not
considering others, especially not considering them as
superior to himself. This feeling of another's superiority
could only be instilled into him by someone who, being
stronger than he is, should force him to give up some
desire, to restrict himself, to restrain himself. He would
then have learned this fundamental discipline: "Here I end
and here begins another more powerful than I am. In
the world, apparently, there are two people: I myself and
another superior to me." The ordinary man of past times
was daily taught this elemental wisdom by the world
about him, because it was a world so rudely organised,
that catastrophes were frequent, and there was nothing
in it certain, abundant, stable. But the new masses find
themselves in the presence of a prospect full of possibilities, and furthermore, quite secure, with everything
ready to their hands, independent of any previous efforts
on their part, just as we find the sun in the heavens without our hoisting it up on our shoulders. No human being
thanks another for the air he breathes, for no one has
produced the air for him; it belongs to the sum-total
of what "is there," of which we say "it is natural," because
it never fails. And these spoiled masses are unintelligent
enough to believe that the material and social organisation, placed at their disposition like the air, is of the same
origin, since apparently it never fails them, and is almost
as perfect as the natural scheme of things.

My thesis, therefore, is this: the very perfection with
which the XIXth Century gave an organisation to certain
orders of existence has caused the masses benefited thereby
to consider it, not as an organised, but as a natural sys-

tem. Thus is explained and defined the absurd state of mind revealed by these masses; they are only concerned with their own well-being, and at the same time they remain alien to the cause of that well-being. As they do not see, behind the benefits of civilisation, marvels of invention and construction which can only be maintained by great effort and foresight, they imagine that their role is limited to demanding these benefits peremptorily, as if they were natural rights. In the disturbances caused by scarcity of food, the mob goes in search of bread, and the means it employs is generally to wreck the bakeries. This may serve as a symbol of the attitude adopted, on a greater and more complicated scale, by the masses of to-day towards the civilisation by which they are supported.

7

Noble Life and Common Life, or Effort and Inertia

To start with, we are what our world invites us to be, and the basic features of our soul are impressed upon it by the form of its surroundings as in a mould. Naturally, for our life is no other than our relations with the world around. The general aspect which it presents to us will form the general aspect of our own life. It is for this reason that I stress so much the observation that the world into which the masses of to-day have been born displays features radically new to history. Whereas in past times life for the average man meant finding all around him difficulties, dangers, want, limitations of his destiny, dependence, the new world appears as a sphere of practically limitless possibilities, safe, and independent of anyone. Based on this primary and lasting impression, the mind of every contemporary man will be formed, just as previous minds were formed on the opposite impression. For that basic impression becomes an interior voice which ceaselessly utters certain words in the depths of each individual, and tenaciously suggests to him a definition of life which is, at the same time, a moral imperative. And if the traditional sentiment whispered: "To live is to feel oneself limited, and therefore to have to count with that which limits us," the newest voice shouts: "To live is to meet with no limitation whatever and, consequently, to abandon oneself calmly to one's self. Practically nothing is impossible, nothing is dangerous, and, in principle, nobody is superior to anybody." This basic experience completely modifies the traditional, persistent structure of the mass-man. For the latter always felt himself, by his nature, confronted with material limitations and higher social powers. Such, in his eyes, was life. If he succeeded in improving his situation, if he climbed the social ladder, he attributed this to a piece of fortune which was favourable to him in particular. And if not to this, then to an enormous effort, of which he knew well what it had cost him. In both cases it was a question of an exception to the general character of life and the world; an exception which, as such, was due to some very special cause.

But the modern mass finds complete freedom as its natural, established condition, without any special cause for it. Nothing from outside incites it to recognise limits to itself and, consequently, to refer at all times to other authorities higher than itself. Until lately, the Chinese peasant believed that the welfare of his existence depended on the private virtues which the Emperor was pleased to possess. Therefore, his life was constantly related to this supreme authority on which it depended. *But the man we are now analysing accustoms himself not to appeal from his own to any authority outside him.* He is satisfied with himself exactly as he is. Ingenuously, without any need of being vain, as the most natural thing in the world, he will tend to consider and affirm as good everything he finds within himself: opinions, appetites, preferences, tastes. Why not, if, as we have seen, nothing and nobody force him to realise that he is a second-class man, subject to many limitations, incapable of creating or conserving that very organisation which gives his life the fullness and contentedness on which he bases this assertion of his personality?

The mass-man would never have accepted authority external to himself had not his surroundings violently forced him to do so. As to-day his surroundings do not so force him, the everlasting mass-man, true to his character, ceases to appeal to other authority and feels himself lord of his own existence. On the contrary the select man, the excellent man is urged, by interior necessity, to appeal from himself to some standard beyond himself, superior to himself, whose service he freely accepts. Let us recall that at the start we distinguished the excellent man from the common man by saying that the former is the one who makes great demands on himself, and the latter the one who makes no demands on himself, but contents himself with what he is, and is delighted with himself.[1] Contrary to what is usually thought, it is the man of excellence, and not the common man who lives in essential servitude. Life has no savour for him unless he makes it consist in service to something transcendental. Hence he does not look upon the necessity of serving as an oppression. When, by chance, such necessity is lacking, he grows restless and invents some new standard, more difficult, more exigent, with which to coerce himself. This is life lived as a discipline—the noble life. Nobility is defined by the demands it makes on us—by obligations, not by rights. *Noblesse oblige.* "To live as one likes is plebeian; the noble man aspires to order and law" (Goethe). The privileges of nobility are not in their origin concessions or favours; on the contrary, they are conquests. And their maintenance supposes, in principle, that the privileged individual is capable of reconquering them, at any moment, if it were

[1] That man is intellectually of the mass who, in face of any problem, is satisfied with thinking the first thing he finds in his head. On the contrary, the excellent man is he who contemns what he finds in his mind without previous effort, and only accepts as worthy of him what is still far above him and what requires a further effort in order to be reached.

necessary, and anyone were to dispute them.[1] Private rights or *privileges* are not, then, passive possession and mere enjoyment, but they represent the standard attained by personal effort. On the other hand, common rights, such as those "of the man and the citizen," are passive property, pure usufruct and benefit, the generous gift of fate which every man finds before him, and which answers to no effort whatever, unless it be that of breathing and avoiding insanity. I would say, then, that an impersonal right is held, a personal one is upheld.

It is annoying to see the degeneration suffered in ordinary speech by a word so inspiring as "nobility." For, by coming to mean for many people hereditary "noble blood," it is changed into something similar to common rights, into a static, passive quality which is received and transmitted like something inert. But the strict sense, the *etymon* of the word nobility is essentially dynamic. Noble means the "well known," that is, known by everyone, famous, he who has made himself known by excelling the anonymous mass. It implies an unusual effort as the cause of his fame. Noble, then, is equivalent to effortful, excellent. The nobility or fame of the son is pure benefit. The son is known because the father made himself famous. He is known by reflection, and in fact, hereditary nobility has an indirect character, it is mirrored light, lunar nobility, something derived from the dead. The only thing left to it of living, authentic, dynamic is the impulse it stirs in the descendant to maintain the level of effort reached by the ancestor. Always, even in this altered sense, *noblesse oblige*. The original noble lays an obligation on himself, the noble heir receives the obligation with his inheritance, but in any case there is a certain contradiction in the passing-on of nobility from the first noble to his successors. The Chinese, more logical, invert

[1] Vide *España Invertebrada* (1922), p. 156.

the order of transmission; it is not the father who ennobles the son, but the son who, by acquiring noble rank, communicates it to his forebears, by his personal efforts bringing fame to his humble stock. Hence, when granting degrees of nobility, they are graduated by the number of previous generations which are honoured; there are those who ennoble only their fathers, and those who stretch back their fame to the fifth or tenth grandparent. The ancestors live by reason of the actual man, whose nobility is effective, active—in a word: *is* not *was*.[1]

"Nobility" does not appear as a formal expression until the Roman Empire, and then precisely in opposition to the hereditary nobles, then in decadence.

 For me, then, nobility is synonymous with a life of effort, ever set on excelling oneself, in passing beyond what one is to what one sets up as a duty and an obligation. In this way the noble life stands opposed to the common or inert life, which reclines statically upon itself, condemned to perpetual immobility, unless an external force compels it to come out of itself. Hence we apply the term mass to this kind of man—not so much because of his multitude as because of his inertia.

As one advances in life, one realises more and more that the majority of men—and of women—are incapable of any other effort than that strictly imposed on them as a reaction to external compulsion. And for that reason, the few individuals we have come across who are capable of a spontaneous and joyous effort stand out isolated, monumentalised, so to speak, in our experience. These are the select men, the nobles, the only ones who are active and not merely reactive, for whom life is a perpetual striving,

[1] As in the foregoing it is only a matter of bringing the word "nobility" back to its original sense which excludes inheritance, this is not the place to study the fact that a "nobility of blood" makes its appearance so often in history. This question, then, is left untouched.

an incessant course of training. Training = *askesis*. These are the ascetics.[1] This apparent digression should not cause surprise. In order to define the actual mass-man, who is as much "mass" as ever, but who wishes to supplant the "excellent," it has been necessary to contrast him with the two pure forms which are mingled in him: the normal mass and the genuine noble or man of effort.

Now we can advance more rapidly, because we are now in possession of what, to my thinking, is the key— the psychological equation—of the human type dominant to-day. All that follows is a consequence, a corollary, of that root-structure, which may be summed up thus: the world as organised by the XIXth Century, when automatically producing a new man, has infused into him formidable appetites and powerful means of every kind for satisfying them. These include the economic, the physical (hygiene, average health higher than any preceding age), the civil and the technical (by which I mean the enormous quantity of partial knowledge and practical efficiency possessed by the average man to-day and lacking to him in the past). After having supplied him with all these powers, the XIXth Century has abandoned him to himself, and the average man, following his natural disposition, has withdrawn into himself. Hence, we are in presence of a mass stronger than that of any preceding period, but differing from the traditional type in that it remains hermetically enclosed within itself, incapable of submitting to anything or anybody, believing itself self-sufficient—in a word, indocile.[2] If things go on as they are at present, it will be every day more noticeable in Europe —and by reflection, throughout the whole world—that

[1] Vide "El Origen deportivo del Estado," in *El Espectador*, VII, recently published.

[2] On the indocility of the masses, especially of the Spanish masses, I have already spoken in *España Invertebrada* (1922), and I refer the reader to what is there said.

the masses are incapable of submitting to direction of any kind. In the difficult times that are at hand for our continent, it is possible that, under a sudden affliction, they may for a moment have the good will to accept, in certain specially urgent matters, the direction of the superior minorities.

But even that good will will result in failure. For the basic texture of their soul is wrought of hermetism and indocility; they are from birth deficient in the faculty of giving attention to what is outside themselves, be it fact or person. They will wish to follow someone, and they will be unable. They will want to listen, and will discover they are deaf.

On the other hand, it is illusory to imagine that the mass-man of to-day, however superior his vital level may be compared with that of other times, will be able to control, by himself, the process of civilisation. I say process, and not progress. The simple process of preserving our present civilisation is supremely complex, and demands incalculably subtle powers. Ill-fitted to direct it is this average man who has learned to use much of the machinery of civilisation, but who is characterised by root-ignorance of the very principles of that civilisation.

I reiterate to the reader who has patiently followed me up to this point, the importance of not giving to the facts enunciated a primarily political significance. On the contrary, political activities, of all those in public life the most efficient and the most visible, are the final product of others more intimate, more impalpable. Hence, political indocility would not be so grave did it not proceed from a deeper, more decisive intellectual indocility. In consequence, until we have analysed this latter, the thesis of this essay will not stand out in its final clarity.

8

Why the Masses Intervene in Everything, and Why Their Intervention Is Solely by Violence

WE TAKE it, then, that there has happened something supremely paradoxical, but which was in truth most natural; from the very opening-out of the world and of life for the average man, his soul has shut up within him. Well, then, I maintain that it is in this obliteration of the average soul that the rebellion of the masses consists, and in this in its turn lies the gigantic problem set before humanity to-day.

I know well that many of my readers do not think as I do. This also is most natural and confirms the theorem. For although my opinion turn out erroneous, there will always remain the fact that many of those dissentient readers have never given five minutes' thought to this complex matter. How are they going to think as I do? But by believing that they have a right to an opinion on the matter without previous effort to work one out for themselves, they prove patently that they belong to that absurd type of human being which I have called the "rebel mass." It is precisely what I mean by having one's soul obliterated, hermetically closed. Here it would be the

special case of intellectual hermetism. The individual finds
himself already with a stock of ideas. He decides to content himself with them and to consider himself intellectually complete. As he feels the lack of nothing outside
himself, he settles down definitely amid his mental furni-
ture. Such is the mechanism of self-obliteration.

The mass-man regards himself as perfect. The select
man, in order to regard himself so, needs to be specially
vain, and the belief in his perfection is not united with
him consubstantially, it is not ingenuous, but arises from
his vanity, and even for himself has a fictitious, imaginary, problematic character. Hence the vain man stands
in need of others, he seeks in them support for the idea
that he wishes to have of himself. So that not even in
this diseased state, not even when blinded by vanity,
does the "noble" man succeed in feeling himself as in
truth complete. Contrariwise, it never occurs to the mediocre man of our days, to the New Adam, to doubt of
his own plenitude. His self-confidence is, like Adam's,
paradisiacal. The innate hermetism of his soul is an obstacle to the necessary condition for his discovery of his
insufficiency, namely: a comparison of himself with other
beings. To compare himself would mean to go out of himself for a moment and to transfer himself to his neighbour.
But the mediocre soul is incapable of transmigrations—
the supreme form of sport.

We find ourselves, then, met with the same difference
that eternally exists between the fool and the man of
sense. The latter is constantly catching himself within an
inch of being a fool; hence he makes an effort to escape
from the imminent folly, and in that effort lies his intelligence. The fool, on the other hand, does not suspect
himself; he thinks himself the most prudent of men, hence
the enviable tranquillity with which the fool settles down,
instals himself in his own folly. Like those insects which

lack of self awareness

can the man of fool become a man of sense?

Is he right in claiming this?

it is impossible to extract from the orifice they inhabit, there is no way of dislodging the fool from his folly, to take him away for a while from his blind state and to force him to contrast his own dull vision with other keener forms of sight. The fool is a fool for life; he is devoid of pores. This is why Anatole France said that the fool is much worse than the knave, for the knave does take a rest sometimes, the fool never.[1]

It is not a question of the mass-man being a fool. On the contrary, to-day he is more clever, has more capacity of understanding than his fellow of any previous period. But that capacity is of no use to him; in reality, the vague feeling that he possesses it seems only to shut him up more within himself and keep him from using it. Once for all, he accepts the stock of commonplaces, prejudices, fag-ends of ideas or simply empty words which chance has piled up within his mind, and with a boldness only explicable by his ingenuousness, is prepared to impose them everywhere. This is what in my first chapter I laid down as the characteristic of our time; not that the vulgar believes itself super-excellent and not vulgar, but that the vulgar proclaims and imposes the rights of vulgarity, or vulgarity as a right.

The command over public life exercised to-day by the intellectually vulgar is perhaps the factor of the present situation which is most novel, least assimilable to anything in the past. At least in European history up to the present, the vulgar had never believed itself to have "ideas" on things. It had beliefs, traditions, experiences, proverbs,

[1] I have often asked myself the following question. There is no doubt that at all times for many men one of the greatest tortures of their lives has been the contact, the collision with the folly of their neighbours. And yet how is it that there has never been attempted—I think this is so—a study on this matter, an Essay on Folly? For the pages of Erasmus do not treat of this aspect of the matter.

WHY THE MASSES INTERVENE   71

mental habits, but it never imagined itself in possession
of theoretical opinions on what things are or ought to be
—for example, on politics or literature. What the politician planned or carried out seemed good or bad to it,
it granted or withheld its support, but its action was
limited to being an echo, positive or negative, of the
creative activity of others. It never occurred to it to oppose to the "ideas" of the politician others of its own, nor
even to judge the politician's "ideas" from the tribunal of
other "ideas" which it believed itself to possess. Similarly
in art and in other aspects of public life. An innate consciousness of its limitation, of its not being qualified to
theorise,[1] effectively prevented it doing so. The necessary consequence of this was that the vulgar never
thought, even remotely, of making a decision on any one
of the public activities, which in their greater part are
theoretical in character. To-day, on the other hand, the
average man has the most mathematical "ideas" on all
that happens or ought to happen in the universe. Hence
he has lost the use of his hearing. Why should he listen
if he has within him all that is necessary? There is no
reason now for listening, but rather for judging, pronouncing, deciding. There is no question concerning public life, in which he does not intervene, blind and deaf as
he is, imposing his "opinions."

But, is this not an advantage? Is it not a sign of immense
progress that the masses should have "ideas," that is to
say, should be cultured? By no means. The "ideas" of
the average man are not genuine ideas, nor is their possession culture. An idea is a putting truth in checkmate.
Whoever wishes to have ideas must first prepare himself
to desire truth and to accept the rules of the game imposed by it. It is no use speaking of ideas when there is

[1] There is no getting away from it; every opinion means setting
up a theory.

no acceptance of a higher authority to regulate them, a series of standards to which it is possible to appeal in a discussion. These standards are the principles on which culture rests. I am not concerned with the form they take. What I affirm is that there is no culture where there are no standards to which our fellow-men can have recourse. There is no culture where there are no principles of legality to which to appeal. There is no culture where there is no acceptance of certain final intellectual positions to which a dispute may be referred.[1] There is no culture where economic relations are not subject to a regulating principle to protect interests involved. There is no culture where aesthetic controversy does not recognise the necessity of justifying the work of art.

When all these things are lacking there is no culture; there is in the strictest sense of the word, barbarism. And let us not deceive ourselves, this is what is beginning to appear in Europe under the progressive rebellion of the masses. The traveller who arrives in a barbarous country knows that in that territory there are no ruling principles to which it is possible to appeal. Properly speaking, there are no barbarian standards. Barbarism is the absence of standards to which appeal can be made.

The varying degrees of culture are measured by the greater or less precision of the standards. Where there is little such precision, these standards rule existence only *grosso modo;* where there is much they penetrate in detail into the exercise of all the activities.[2]

[1] If anyone in a discussion with us is not concerned with adjusting himself to truth, if he has no wish to find the truth, he is intellectually a barbarian. That, in fact, is the position of the mass-man when he speaks, lectures, or writes.

[2] The paucity of Spanish intellectual culture is shown, not in greater or less knowledge, but in the habitual lack of caution and care to adjust one's self to truth which is usually displayed by those who speak and write. It is not the fact of judging rightly or wrongly—truth is not within our reach—but the lack of scruple

Anyone can observe that in Europe, for some years past, "strange things" have begun to happen. To give a concrete example of these "strange things" I shall name certain political movements, such as Syndicalism and Fascism. We must not think that they seem strange simply because they are new. The enthusiasm for novelty is so innate in the European that it has resulted in his producing the most unsettled history of all known to us. The element of strangeness in these new facts is not to be attributed to the element of novelty, but to the extraordinary form taken by these new things. Under the species of Syndicalism and Fascism there appears for the first time in Europe a type of man who does not want to give reasons or to be right, but simply shows himself resolved to impose his opinions. This is the new thing: the right not to be reasonable, the "reason of unreason." [1] Here I see the most palpable manifestation of the new mentality of the masses, due to their having decided to rule society without the capacity for doing so. In their political conduct the structure of the new mentality is revealed in the rawest, most convincing manner; but the key to it lies in intellectual hermetism. The average man finds himself with "ideas" in his head, but he lacks the faculty of ideation. He has no conception even of the rare atmosphere in which ideas live. He wishes to have opinions, but is unwilling to accept the conditions and presuppositions that underlie all opinion. Hence his ideas are in effect nothing more than appetites in words, something like musical romanzas.

To have an idea means believing one is in possession

---

which makes them omit the elementary requirements for right judgment. We are like the country priest who triumphantly refutes the Manichean without having troubled to inquire what the Manichean believes.

[1] The reference is to the well-known phrase in Don Quixote.—TR.

of the reasons for having it, and consequently means believing that there is such a thing as reason, a world of
intelligible truths. To have ideas, to form opinions, is
identical with appealing to such an authority, submitting
oneself to it, accepting its code and its decisions, and
therefore believing that the highest form of intercommunion is the dialogue in which the reasons for our ideas
are discussed. But the mass-man would feel himself lost
if he accepted discussion, and instinctively repudiates the
obligation of accepting that supreme authority lying outside himself. Hence the "new thing" in Europe is "to
have done with discussions," and detestation is expressed
for all forms of intercommunion which imply acceptance
of objective standards, ranging from conversation to Parliament, and taking in science. This means that there is
a renunciation of the common life based on culture, which
is subject to standards, and a return to the common life
of barbarism. All the normal processes are suppressed in
order to arrive directly at the imposition of what is desired. The hermetism of the soul which, as we have seen
before, urges the mass to intervene in the whole of public
life, also inevitably leads it to one single process of intervention: direct action.

When the reconstruction of the origins of our epoch
is undertaken, it will be observed that the first notes of
its special harmony were sounded in those groups of
French syndicalists and realists of about 1900, inventors
of the method and the name of "direct action." Man has
always had recourse to violence; sometimes this recourse
was a mere crime, and does not interest us here. But at
other times violence was the means resorted to by him
who had previously exhausted all others in defence of
the rights of justice which he thought he possessed. It
may be regrettable that human nature tends on occasion
to this form of violence, but it is undeniable that it im-

plies the greatest tribute to reason and justice. For this form of violence is none other than reason exasperated. Force was, in fact, the *ultima ratio*. Rather stupidly it has been the custom to take ironically this expression, which clearly indicates the previous submission of force to methods of reason. Civilisation is nothing else than the attempt to reduce force to being the *ultima ratio*. We are now beginning to realise this with startling clearness, because "direct action" consists in inverting the order and proclaiming violence as *prima ratio*, or strictly as *unica ratio*. It is the norm which proposes the annulment of all norms, which suppresses all intermediate process between our purpose and its execution. It is the Magna Charta of barbarism.

It is well to recall that at every epoch when the mass, for one purpose or another, has taken a part in public life, it has been in the form of "direct action." This was, then, the natural *modus operandi* of the masses. And the thesis of this essay is strongly confirmed by the patent fact that at present when the overruling intervention in public life of the masses has passed from casual and infrequent to being the normal, it is "direct action" which appears officially as the recognized method.

All our communal life is coming under this regime in which appeal to "indirect" authority is suppressed. In social relations "good manners" no longer hold sway. Literature as "direct action" appears in the form of insult. The restrictions of sexual relations are reduced.

Restrictions, standards, courtesy, indirect methods, justice, reason! Why were all these invented, why all these complications created? They are all summed up in the word civilisation, which, through the underlying notion of *civis*, the citizen, reveals its real origin. By means of all these there is an attempt to make possible the city, the community, common life. Hence, if we look into

is civilization or man of intelligence ↗ ⟶ barbarian
or man of fool

is agreeing with a public figure
constitution of being a man
of fool

all these constituents of civilisation just enumerated, we shall find the same common basis. All, in fact, presuppose the radical progressive desire on the part of each individual to take others into consideration. Civilisation is before all, the will to live in common. A man is uncivilised, barbarian in the degree in which he does not take others into account. Barbarism is the tendency to disassociation. Accordingly, all barbarous epochs have been times of human scattering, of the pullulation of tiny groups, separate from and hostile to one another.

The political doctrine which has represented the loftiest endeavour towards common life is liberal democracy. It carries to the extreme the determination to have consideration for one's neighbour and is the prototype of "indirect action." Liberalism is that principle of political rights, according to which the public authority, in spite of being all-powerful, limits itself and attempts, even at its own expense, to leave room in the State over which it rules for those to live who neither think nor feel as it does, that is to say as do the stronger, the majority. Liberalism—it is well to recall this to-day—is the supreme form of generosity; it is the right which the majority concedes to minorities and hence it is the noblest cry that has ever resounded in this planet. It announces the determination to share existence with the enemy; more than that, with an enemy which is weak. It was incredible that the human species should have arrived at so noble an attitude, so paradoxical, so refined, so acrobatic, so anti-natural. Hence, it is not to be wondered at that this same humanity should soon appear anxious to get rid of it. It is a discipline too difficult and complex to take firm root on earth.

Share our existence with the enemy! Govern with the opposition! Is not such a form of tenderness beginning to seem incomprehensible? Nothing indicates more clearly the characteristics of the day than the fact that there are so few countries where an opposition exists. In almost all, a homogeneous mass weighs on public authority and crushes down, annihilates every opposing group. The mass—who would credit it as one sees its compact, multitudinous appearance?—does not wish to share life with those who are not of it. It has a deadly hatred of all that is not itself.

9

The Primitive and the Technical

It is much to my purpose to recall that we are here engaged in the analysis of a situation—the actual one—which is of its essence ambiguous. Hence I suggested at the start that all the features of the present day, and in particular the rebellion of the masses, offer a double aspect. Any one of them not only admits of, but requires, a double interpretation, favourable and unfavourable. And this ambiguity lies, not in our minds, but in the reality itself. It is not that the present situation may appear to us good from one view-point, and evil from another, but that in itself it contains the twin potencies of triumph or of death.

There is no call to burden this essay with a complete philosophy of history. But it is evident that I am basing it on the underlying foundation of my own philosophical convictions. I do not believe in the absolute determinism of history. On the contrary, I believe that all life, and consequently the life of history, is made up of simple moments, each of them relatively undetermined in respect of the previous one, so that in it reality hesitates, walks up and down, and is uncertain whether to decide for one or other of various possibilities. It is this metaphysical hesitancy which gives to everything living its unmistakable character of tremulous vibration. The rebellion of

78

the masses *may*, in fact, be the transition to some new, un-exampled organisation of humanity, but it *may* also be a catastrophe of human destiny. There is no reason to deny the reality of progress, but there is to correct the notion that believes this progress secure. It is more in accordance with facts to hold that there is no certain progress, no evolution, without the threat of "involution," of retrogression. Everything is possible in history; tri-umphant, indefinite progress equally with periodic retro-gression. For life, individual or collective, personal or his-toric, is the one entity in the universe whose substance is compact of danger, of adventure. It is, in the strict sense of the word, drama.[1]

This, which is true in general, acquires greater force in "moments of crisis" such as the present. And so, the symptoms of new conduct which are appearing under the actual dominion of the masses, and which we have grouped under the term "direct action," *may* also announce future perfections. It is evident that every old civilisation drags with it in its advance worn-out tissues and no small load of callous matter, which form an obstacle to life, mere

---

[1] Needless to say, hardly anyone will take seriously these expres-sions, and even the best-intentioned will understand them as mere metaphors, though perhaps striking ones. Only an odd reader, ingenuous enough not to believe that he already knows definitively what life is, or at least what it is not, will allow himself to be won over by the primary meaning of these phrases, and will be precisely the one who will *understand* them—be they true or false. Amongst the rest there will reign the most effusive unanim-ity, with this solitary difference: some will think that, *speaking seriously*, life is the process of existence of a soul, and others that it is a succession of chemical reactions. I do not conceive that it will improve my position with readers so hermetically sealed to resume my whole line of thought by saying that the *primary, radical* meaning of life appears when it is employed in the sense not of biology, but of biography. For the very strong reason that the whole of biology is quite definitely only a chapter in certain biographies, it is what biologists do in the portion of their lives open to biography. Anything else is abstraction, fantasy and myth.

toxic dregs. There are dead institutions, valuations and estimates which still survive, though now meaningless, unnecessarily complicated solutions, standards whose lack of substance has been proved. All these constituents of "indirect action," of civilisation, demand a period of feverish simplification. The tall hat and frock-coat of the romantic period are avenged by means of present-day *déshabillé* and "shirt-sleeves." Here, the simplification means hygiene and better taste, consequently a more perfect solution, as always happens when more is obtained by smaller means. The tree of romantic love also was badly in need of pruning in order to shed the abundance of imitation magnolias tacked on to its branches and the riot of creepers, spirals, and tortuous ramifications which deprived it of the sun.

In general, public life and above all politics, urgently needed to be brought back to reality, and European humanity could not turn the somersault which the optimist demands of it, without first taking off its clothes, getting down to its bare essence, returning to its real self. The enthusiasm which I feel for this discipline of stripping oneself bare, of being one's real self, the belief that it is indispensable in order to clear the way to a worthy future, leads me to claim full liberty of thought with regard to everything in the past. It is the future which must prevail over the past, and from it we take our orders regarding our attitude towards what has been.[1]

[1] This freedom of attitude towards the past is not, then, a peevish revolt, but, on the contrary, an evident obligation, on the part of every "period of criticism." If I defend the liberalism of the XIXth Century against the masses which rudely attack it, this does not mean that I renounce my full freedom of opinion as regards that same liberalism. And vice versa, the primitivism which in this essay appears in its worst aspect is in a certain sense a condition of every great historic advance. Compare what, a few years ago, I said on this matter in the essay "Biología y Pedagogía" (*El Espectador*, III, *La paradoja del salvajismo*).

But it is necessary to avoid the great sin of those who directed the XIXth Century, the lack of recognition of their responsibilities which prevented them from keeping alert and on the watch. To let oneself slide down the easy slope offered by the course of events and to dull one's mind against the extent of the danger, the unpleasant features which characterise even the most joyous hour, that is precisely to fail in one's obligation of responsibility. To-day it has become necessary to stir up an exaggerated sense of responsibility in those capable of feeling it, and it seems of supreme urgency to stress the evidently dangerous aspect of present-day symptoms.

There is no doubt that on striking a balance of our public life the adverse factors far outweigh the favourable ones, if the calculation be made not so much in regard to the present, as to what they announce and promise for the future.

All the increased material possibilities which life has experienced run the risk of being annulled when they are faced with the staggering problem that has come upon the destiny of Europe, and which I once more formulate: the direction of society has been taken over by a type of man who is not interested in the principles of civilisation. Not of this or that civilisation but—from what we can judge to-day—of any civilisation. Of course, he is interested in anesthetics, motor-cars, and a few other things. But this fact merely confirms his fundamental lack of interest in civilisation. For those things are merely its products, and the fervour with which he greets them only brings into stronger relief his indifference to the principles from which they spring. It is sufficient to bring forward this fact: since the *nuove scienze*, the natural sciences, came into being—from the Renaissance on, that is to say—the enthusiasm for them had gone on increasing through the course of time. To put it more concretely, the proportionate number of people who devoted themselves to pure scientific research was in each generation greater. The first case of retrogression—relative, I repeat—has occurred in the generation of those between twenty and thirty at the present time. It is becoming difficult to attract students to the laboratories of pure science. And this is happening when industry is reaching its highest stage of development, and when people in general are showing still greater appetite for the use of the apparatus and the medicines created by science. If we did not wish to avoid prolixity, similar incongruity could be shown in politics, art, morals, religion, and in the everyday activities of life.

What is the significance to us of so paradoxical a situation? This essay is an attempt to prepare the answer to that question. The meaning is that the type of man dominant to-day is a primitive one, a *Naturmensch* rising up in the midst of a civilised world. The world is a civilised one, its inhabitant is not: he does not see the civilisation of the world around him, but he uses it as if it were a natural force. The new man wants his motor-car, and enjoys it, but he believes that it is the spontaneous fruit of an Edenic tree. In the depths of his soul he is unaware of the artificial, almost incredible, character of civilisation, and does not extend his enthusiasm for the instruments to the principles which make them possible. When some pages back, by a transposition of the words of Rathenau, I said that we are witnessing the "vertical invasion of the barbarians" it might be thought (it generally is) that it was only a matter of a "phrase." It is now clear that the expression may enshrine a truth or an error, but that it is the very opposite of a "phrase," namely: a formal definition which sums up a whole complicated analysis. The actual mass-man is, in fact, a primitive who has slipped through the wings on to the age-old stage of civilisation.

There is continual talk to-day of the fabulous progress of technical knowledge; but I see no signs in this talk, even amongst the best, of a sufficiently dramatic realisation of its future. Spengler himself, so subtle and profound—though so subject to mania—appears to me in this matter far too optimistic. For he believes that "culture" is to be succeeded by an era of "civilisation," by which word he understands more especially technical efficiency. The idea that Spengler has of "culture" and of history in general is so remote from that underlying this essay, that it is not easy, even for the purpose of correction, to comment here upon his conclusions. It is only by taking great leaps and neglecting exact details, in order to bring both view-points under a common denominator, that it is possible to indicate the difference between us. Spengler believes that "technicism" can go on living when interest in the principles underlying culture are dead. I cannot bring myself to believe any such thing. Technicism and science are consubstantial, and science no longer exists when it ceases to interest for itself alone, and it cannot so interest unless men continue to feel enthusiasm for the general principles of culture. If this fervour is deadened—as appears to be happening—technicism can only survive for a time, for the duration of the inertia of the cultural impulse which started it. We live with our technical requirements, but not *by* them. These give neither nourishment nor breath to themselves, they are not *causae sui*, but a useful, practical precipitate of superfluous, unpractical activities.[1] I proceed, then, to the position that the actual interest in technical accomplishment guarantees nothing, less than nothing, for the progress or the duration of such accomplishment. It is

[1] Hence, to my mind, a definition of North America by its "technicism" tells us nothing. One of the things that most seriously confuse the European mind is the mass of puerile judgments that one hears pronounced on North America even by the most cultured

quite right that technicism should be considered one of the characteristic features of "modern culture," that is to say, of a culture which comprises a species of science which proves materially profitable. Hence, when describing the newest aspect of the existence implanted by the XIXth Century, I was left with these two features: liberal democracy and technicism. But I repeat that I am astonished at the ease with which when speaking of technicism it is forgotten that its vital centre is pure science, and that the conditions for its continuance involve the same conditions that render possible pure scientific activity. Has any thought been given to the number of things that must remain active in men's souls in order that there may still continue to be "men of science" in real truth? Is it seriously thought that as long as there are dollars there will be science? This notion in which so many find rest is only a further proof of primitivism. As if there were not numberless ingredients, of most disparate nature, to be brought together and shaken up in order to obtain the cocktail of physico-chemical science! Under even the most perfunctory examination of this subject, the evident fact bursts into view that over the whole extent of space and time, physico-chemistry has succeeded in establishing itself completely only in the small quadrilateral enclosed by London, Berlin, Vienna, and Paris, and that only in the XIXth Century. This proves that experimental science is one of the most unlikely products of history. Seers, priests, warriors and shepherds have abounded in all times and places. But this fauna of experimental man apparently requires for its production a combination of circumstances more exceptional than those that engender the unicorn. Such a bare, sober fact should make us re-

persons. This is one particular case of the disproportion which I indicate later on as existing between the complexity of present-day problems and the capacity of present-day minds.

flect a little on the supervolatile, evaporative character of scientific inspiration.[1] Blissful the man who believes that, were Europe to disappear, the North Americans could *continue* science! It would be of great value to treat the matter thoroughly and to specify in detail what are the historical presuppositions, vital to experimental science and, consequently, to technical accomplishment. But let no one hope that, even when this point was made clear, the mass-man would understand. The mass-man has no attention to spare for reasoning, he learns only in his own flesh.

There is one observation which bars me from deceiving myself as to the efficacy of such preachments, which by the fact of being based on reason would necessarily be subtle. Is it not altogether absurd that, under actual circumstances, the average man does not feel spontaneously, and without being preached at, an ardent enthusiasm for those sciences and the related ones of biology? For, just consider what the actual situation is. While evidently all the other constituents of culture—politics, art, social standards, morality itself—have become problematic, there is one which increasingly demonstrates, in a manner most indisputable and most suitable to impress the mass-man, its marvellous efficiency: and that one is empirical science. Every day furnishes a new invention which this average man utilises. Every day produces a new anesthetic or vaccine from which this average man benefits. Everyone knows that, if scientific inspiration does not weaken and the laboratories are multiplied three times or ten times, there will be an automatic multiplication of wealth, comfort, health, prosperity. Can any more

[1] This, without speaking of more internal questions. The majority of the investigators themselves have not to-day the slightest suspicion of the very grave and dangerous internal crisis through which their science is passing.

formidable, more convincing propaganda be imagined in favour of a vital principle? How is it, nevertheless, that there is no sign of the masses imposing on themselves any sacrifice of money or attention in order to endow science more worthily? Far from this being the case, the post-war period has converted the man of science into a new social pariah. And note that I am referring to physicists, chemists, biologists, not to philosophers. Philosophy needs neither protection, attention nor sympathy from the masses. It maintains its character of complete inutility,[1] and thereby frees itself from all subservience to the average man. It recognises itself as essentially problematic, and joyously accepts its free destiny as a bird of the air, without asking anybody to take it into account, without recommending or defending itself. If it does really turn out to the advantage of anyone, it rejoices from simple human sympathy; but does not live on the profit it brings to others, neither anticipating it nor hoping for it. How can it lay claim to being taken seriously by anyone if it starts off by doubting its own existence, if it lives only in the measure in which it combats itself, deprives itself of life? Let us, then, leave out of the question philosophy, which is an adventure of another order. But the experimental sciences do need the cooperation of the mass-man, just as he needs them, under pain of dissolution, inasmuch as in a planet without physico-chemistry the number of beings existing to-day cannot be sustained.

What arguments can bring about something which has not been brought about by the motor-car in which those men come and go, and the pantopon injection which destroys, *miraculously*, their pains? The disproportion between the constant, evident benefit which science procures them and the interest they show in it is such that it is impossible to-day to deceive oneself with illusory

[1] Aristotle, *Metaphysics*, 893a. 10.

hopes and to expect anything but barbarism from those who so behave. *Especially if, as we shall see, this disregard of science as such appears, with possibly more evidence than elsewhere, in the mass of technicians themselves—doctors, engineers, etc.*, who are in the habit of exercising their profession in a state of mind identical in all essentials to that of the man who is content to use his motor-car or buy his tube of aspirin—without the slightest intimate solidarity with the future of science, of civilisation.

There may be those who feel more disturbed by other symptoms of emergent barbarism which, being positive in quality, results of action and not of omission, strike the attention more, materialise into a spectacle. For myself, this matter of the disproportion between the profit which the average man draws from science and the gratitude which he returns—or, rather, does not return—to it; this is much more terrifying.[1] I can only succeed in explaining to myself this absence of adequate recognition by recalling that in Central Africa the negroes also ride in motor-cars and dose themselves with aspirin. The European who is beginning to predominate—so runs my hypothesis—must then be, *in relation to the complex civilisation into which he has been born,* a primitive man, a barbarian appearing on the stage through the trap-door, a "vertical invader."

[1] The monstrosity is increased a hundredfold by the fact that, as I have indicated, all the other vital principles, politics, law, art, morals, religion, are actually passing through a crisis, are at least temporarily bankrupt. Science alone is not bankrupt; rather does it every day pay out, with fabulous interest, all and more than it promises. It is, then, without a competitor; it is impossible to excuse the average man's disregard of it by considering him distracted from it by some other cultural enthusiasm.

10

Primitivism and History

NATURE is always with us. It is self-supporting. In the forests of Nature we can be savages with impunity. We can likewise resolve never to cease being so, without further risk than the coming of other peoples who are not savages. But, in principle, it is possible to have peoples who are perennially primitive. Breyssig has called these "the peoples of perpetual dawn," those who have remained in a motionless, frozen twilight, which never progresses towards midday.

This is what happens in the world which is mere Nature. But it does not happen in the world of civilisation which is ours. Civilisation is not "just there," it is not self-supporting. It is artificial and requires the artist or the artisan. If you want to make use of the advantages of civilisation, but are not prepared to concern yourself with the upholding of civilisation—you are done. In a trice you find yourself left without civilisation. Just a slip, and when you look around everything has vanished into air. The primitive forest appears in its native state, just as if curtains covering pure Nature had been drawn back. The jungle is always primitive and, vice versa, everything primitive is mere jungle.

The romantics of every period have been excited by those scenes of violation, in which the natural and infrahuman assaults the white form of woman, and they have depicted Leda and the swan, Pasiphae and the bull, Antiope and the goat. Generalising the picture, they have

88

found a more subtly indecent spectacle in the landscape with ruins, where the civilised, geometric stone is stifled beneath the embrace of wild vegetation. When your good romantic catches sight of a building, the first thing his eyes seek is the yellow hedge-mustard on cornice and roof. This proclaims, that in the long run, everything is earth, that the jungle springs up everywhere anew. It would be stupid to laugh at the romantic. The romantic *also* is in the right. Under these innocently perverse images there lies an immense, ever-present problem: that of the relations between civilisation and what lies behind it—Nature, between the rational and the cosmic. I reserve, then, the right to deal with this subject on another occasion and to be a romantic myself at an opportune moment.

But just now I am engaged in a contrary task. It is a question of keeping back the invading jungle. The "good European" must at present busy himself with something similar to what caused grave concern to the Australian states: how to prevent the prickly-pear from gaining ground and driving man into the sea. Some time in the forties a Mediterranean emigrant, homesick for his native scenery—Malaga, Sicily?—took with him to Australia a pot with a wretched little prickly-pear. To-day the Australian budgets are weighed down with the burden of charges for the war against the prickly-pear, which has invaded the continent and each year advances over a square kilometre of ground.

The mass-man believes that the civilisation into which he was born and which he makes use of, is as spontaneous and self-producing as Nature, and *ipso facto* he is changed into primitive man. For him, civilisation is the forest. This I have said before; now I have to treat it in more detail.

The principles on which the civilised world—which has

to be maintained—is based, simply do not exist for the average man of to-day. He has no interest in the basic cultural values, no solidarity with them, is not prepared to place himself at their service. How has this come about? For many reasons, but for the moment I am only going to stress one. Civilisation becomes more complex and difficult in proportion as it advances. The problems which it sets before us to-day are of the most intricate. The number of people whose minds are equal to these problems becomes increasingly smaller. The post-war period offers us a striking example of this. The reconstruction of Europe—as we are seeing—is an affair altogether too algebraical, and the ordinary European is showing himself below this high enterprise. It is not that means are lacking for the solution. What are lacking are heads. Or, rather, there are some heads, very few, but the average mass of Central Europe is unwilling to place them on its shoulders.

This disproportion between the complex subtlety of the problems and the minds that should study them will become greater if a remedy be not found, and it constitutes the basic tragedy of our civilisation. By reason of the very fertility and certainty of its formative principles, its production increases in quantity and in subtlety, so as to exceed the receptive powers of normal man. I do not think that this has ever happened in the past. All previous civilisations have died through the insufficiency of their underlying principles. That of Europe is beginning to succumb for the opposite reason. In Greece and Rome it was not man that failed, but principles. The Roman Empire came to an end for lack of technique. When it reached a high level of population, and this vast community demanded the solution of certain material problems which technique only could furnish, the ancient world started on a process of involution, retrogression, and decay.

But to-day it is man who is the failure, because he is unable to keep pace with the progress of his own civilisation. It is painful to hear relatively cultured people speak concerning the most elementary problems of the day. They seem like rough farmhands trying with thick, clumsy fingers to pick up a needle lying on a table. Political and social subjects, for example, are handled with the same rude instruments of thought which served two hundred years since to tackle situations in effect two hundred times less complex.

Advanced civilisation is one and the same thing as arduous problems. Hence, the greater the progress, the greater danger it is in. Life gets gradually better, but evidently also gradually more complicated. Of course, as problems become more complex, the means of solving them also become more perfect. But each new generation must master these perfected means. Amongst them —to come to the concrete—there is one most plainly attached to the advance of a civilisation, namely, that it háve a great deal of the past at its back, a great deal of experience; in a word: history. Historical knowledge is a technique of the first order to preserve and continue a civilisation already advanced. Not that it affords positive solutions to the new aspect of vital conditions—life is always different from what it was—but that it prevents us committing the ingenuous mistakes of other times. But if, in addition to being old and, therefore, beginning to find life difficult, you have lost the memory of the past, and do not profit by experience, then everything turns to disadvantage. Well, it is my belief that this is the situation of Europe. The most "cultured" people to-day are suffering from incredible ignorance of history. I maintain that at the present day, European leaders know much less history than their fellows of the XVIIIth, even of the XVIIth Century. That historical knowledge of the governing minorities—governing *sensu lato*—made possible the prodigious advance of the XIXth Century. Their policy was thought out—by the XVIIIth Century—precisely in order to avoid the errors of previous politics, thought out in view of those errors and embraced in its substance the whole extent of experience. But the XIXth Century already began to lose "historic culture," although during the century the specialists gave it notable advance as a science.[1] To this neglect is due in great part its peculiar errors, which to-day press upon us. In the last third of the century there began—though hidden from sight—that involution, that retrogression towards barbarism, that is, towards the ingenuousness and primitivism of the man who has no past, or who has forgotten it.

Hence, Bolshevism and Fascism, the two "new" attempts in politics that are being made in Europe and on its borders, are two clear examples of essential retrogression. Not so much by the positive content of their doctrine, which, taken in isolation, naturally has its partial truth—what is there in the universe which has not some particle of truth?—as on account of the *anti*-historic, anachronistic way in which they handle the rational elements which the doctrine contains. Typical movements of mass-men, directed, as all such are, by men who are mediocrities, improvised, devoid of a long memory and a "historic conscience," they behave from the start as if they already belonged to the past, as if, though occurring at the present hour, they were really fauna of a past age.

It is not a question of being, or not being, a Com-

---

[1] Here we catch a glimpse of the difference we shall shortly have to treat of between the state of the sciences during a given period and the state of its culture.

munist or a Bolshevist. I am not discussing the creed. What is inconceivable and anachronistic is that a Communist of 1917 should launch out into a revolution which is identical in form with all those which have gone before, and in which there is not the slightest amendment of the defects and errors of its predecessors. Hence, what has happened in Russia possesses no historic interest, it is, strictly speaking, anything but a new start in human life. On the contrary, it is a monotonous repetition of the eternal revolution, it is the perfect commonplace of revolutions. To such an extent, that there is not one stock-phrase of the many that human experience has produced regarding revolutions which does not receive distressful confirmation when applied to this one. "Revolution devours its own children." "Revolution starts from a moderate party, proceeds to the extremists, and soon begins to fall back on some form of restoration," etc., etc. To these venerable commonplaces might be added other truths less well known, though no less probable, amongst them this one: a revolution does not last more than fifteen years, the period which coincides with the flourishing of a generation.[1]

Whoever aspires to create a new social or political reality must before all concern himself to ensure that these humble commonplaces of historical experience will

[1] A generation lasts about thirty years. But its activity divides into two stages and takes two forms: during approximately one half, the new generation carries out the propaganda of its ideas, preferences, and tastes, which finally arrive at power and are dominant in the second half or its course. But the generation educated under its sway is already bringing forward other ideas, preferences, and tastes, which it begins to diffuse in the general atmosphere. When the ideas, preferences, and tastes of the ruling generation are extremist, and therefore revolutionary, those of the new generation are anti-extremist and anti-revolutionary, that is to say, substantially restorationist in spirit. Of course, by restorationist is not to be understood a simple "return to the old ways," a thing which restorations have never been.

be invalidated by the situation which he brings into being. For my part, I shall reserve the title of "man of genius" for the politician who has hardly begun his operations when the professors of history in our colleges begin to go mad, as they see all the "laws" of their science interrupted in their action, falling to pieces, reduced to dust.

By changing the sign proper to Bolshevism, we might make similar statements in regard to Fascism. Neither of these experiments is "at the height of our time." They do not represent the whole of the past in foreshortening, a condition which is essential in order to improve on that past. The struggle with the past is not a hand-to-hand fight. The future overcomes it by swallowing it. If it leaves anything outside it is lost.

Both Bolshevism and Fascism are two false dawns; they do not bring the morning of a new day, but of some archaic day, spent over and over again: they are mere primitivism. And such will all movements be which fall into the stupidity of starting a boxing-match with some portion or other of the past, instead of proceeding to digest it. No doubt an advance must be made on the liberalism of the XIXth Century. But this is precisely what cannot be done by any movement such as Fascism, which declares itself anti-liberal. Because it was that fact —the being anti-liberal or non-liberal—which constituted man previous to liberalism. And as the latter triumphed over its opposite, it will either repeat its victory time and again, or else everything—liberalism and anti-liberalism —will be annihilated in the destruction of Europe. There is an inexorable chronology of life. In it liberalism is posterior to anti-liberalism, or what comes to the same, is more vital than it, just as the gun is more of a weapon than the lance.

At first sight, an attitude "anti-anything" seems posterior to this thing, inasmuch as it signifies a reaction against it and supposes its previous existence. But the innovation which the *anti* represents fades away into an empty negative attitude, leaving as its only positive content an "antique." When his attitude is translated into positive language, the man who declares himself anti-Peter does nothing more than declare himself the upholder of a world where Peter is non-existent. But that is exactly what happened to the world before Peter was born. The anti-Peterite, instead of placing himself after Peter, makes himself previous to him and reverses the whole film to the situation of the past, at the end of which the re-apparition of Peter is inevitable. The same thing happens to these *antis* as, according to the legend, happened to Confucius. He was born, naturally, after his father, but he was born at the age of eighty, while his progenitor was only thirty! Every *anti* is nothing more than a simple, empty *No*.

This would be all very nice and fine if with a good, round *No* we could annihilate the past. But the past is of its essence a *revenant*. If put out, it comes back, inevitably. Hence, the only way to separate from it is not to put it out, but to accept its existence, and so to behave in regard to it as to dodge it, to avoid it. In a word, to live "at the height of our time," with an exaggerated consciousness of the historical circumstances.

The past has reason on its side, its own reason. If that reason is not admitted, it will return to demand it. Liberalism had its reason, which will have to be admitted *per saecula saeculorum*. But it had not the whole of reason, and it is that part which was not reason that must be taken from it. Europe needs to preserve its essential liberalism. This is the condition for superseding it.

If I have spoken here of Fascism and Bolshevism it has been only indirectly, considering merely their aspect as anachronisms. This aspect is, to my mind, inseparable from all that is apparently triumphant to-day. For to-day it is the mass-man who triumphs, and consequently, only those designs inspired by him, saturated with his primitive style, can enjoy an apparent victory. But apart from this, I am not at present discussing the true inwardness of one or the other, just as I am not attempting to solve the eternal dilemma of revolution and evolution. The most that this essay dares to demand is that the revolution or the evolution be historical and not anachronistic.

The theme I am pursuing in these pages is politically neutral, because it breathes an air much ampler than that of politics and its dissensions. Conservative and Radical are none the less mass, and the difference between them —which at every period has been very superficial—does not in the least prevent them both being one and the same man—the common man in rebellion.

There is no hope for Europe unless its destiny is placed in the hands of men really "contemporaneous," men who feel palpitating beneath them the whole subsoil of history, who realise the present level of existence, and abhor every archaic and primitive attitude. We have need of history in its entirety, not to fall back into it, but to see if we can escape from it.

11

The Self-Satisfied Age

To RESUME; the new social fact here analysed is this: European history reveals itself, for the first time, as handed over to the decisions of the ordinary man as such. Or to turn it into the active voice: the ordinary man, hitherto guided by others, has resolved to govern the world himself. This decision to advance to the social foreground has been brought about in him automatically, when the new type of man he represents had barely arrived at maturity. If from the view-point of what concerns public life, the psychological structure of this new type of mass-man be studied, what we find is as follows: (1) An inborn, root-impression that life is easy, plentiful, without any grave limitations; consequently, each average man finds within himself a sensation of power and triumph which, (2) invites him to stand up for himself as he is, to look upon his moral and intellectual endowment as excellent, complete. This contentment with himself leads him to shut himself off from any external court of appeal; not to listen, not to submit his opinions to judgment, not to consider others' existence. His intimate feeling of power urges him always to exercise predominance. He will act then as if he and his like were the only beings existing in the world; and, consequently, (3) will intervene in all matters, imposing his own vulgar views without respect or regard for others, without limit or reserve, that is to say, in accordance with a system of "direct action."

It was this series of aspects which made us think of

certain defective types of humanity, such as the spoiled child, and the primitive in revolt, that is, the barbarian. (The normal primitive, on the other hand, is the most submissive to external authority ever known, be it religion, taboo, social tradition, or customs.) There is no need to be surprised at my heaping up hard names against this type of human being. This present essay is nothing more than a preliminary skirmish against this triumphant man, and the announcement that a certain number of Europeans are about to turn energetically against his attempt to tyrannise. For the moment it is only a first skirmish, the frontal attack will come later, perhaps very soon, and in a very different form from that adopted by this essay. The frontal attack must come in such a way that the massman cannot take precautions against it; he will see it before him and will not suspect that it precisely is the frontal attack.

This type which at present is to be found everywhere, and everywhere imposes his own spiritual barbarism, is, in fact, the spoiled child of human history. The spoiled child is the heir who behaves exclusively as a mere heir. In this case the inheritance is civilisation—with its conveniences, its security; in a word, with all its advantages. As we have seen, it is only in circumstances of easy existence such as our civilisation has produced, that a type can arise, marked by such a collection of features, inspired by such a character. It is one of a number of deformities produced by luxury in human material. There might be a deceptive tendency to believe that a life born into a world of plenty should be better, more really a life than one which consists in a struggle against scarcity. Such is not the case, for reasons of the strictest and most fundamental nature, which this is not the place to enlarge upon. For the present, instead of those reasons, it is sufficient to recall the ever-recurrent fact which constitutes the tragedy of every hereditary aristocracy. The aristocrat inherits, that is to say, he finds attributed to his person, conditions of life which he has not created, and which, therefore, are not produced in organic union with his personal, individual existence. At birth he finds himself installed, suddenly and without knowing how, in the midst of his riches and his prerogatives. In his own self, he has nothing to do with them, because they do not come from him. They are the giant armour of some other person, some other human being, his ancestor. And he has to live as an heir, that is to say, he has to wear the trappings of another existence. What does this bring us to? What life is the "aristocrat" by inheritance going to lead, his own or that of his first noble ancestor? Neither one nor the other. He is condemned to *represent* the other man, consequently, to *be* neither that other nor himself. Inevitably his life loses all authenticity, and is transformed into pure representation or fiction of another life. The abundance of resources that he is obliged to make use of gives him no chance to live out his own personal destiny, his life is atrophied. *All life is the struggle, the effort to be itself.* The difficulties which I meet with in order to realise my existence are precisely what awaken and mobilise my activities, my capacities. If my body was not a weight to me, I should not be able to walk. If the atmosphere did not press on me, I should feel my body as something vague, flabby, unsubstantial. So in the "aristocratic" heir his whole individuality grows vague, for lack of use and vital effort. The result is that specific stupidity of "our old nobility" which is unlike anything else—a stupidity which, strictly speaking, has never yet been described in its intimate, tragic mechanism —that tragic mechanism which leads all hereditary aristocracy to irremediable degeneration.

So much merely to counteract our ingenuous tendency

to believe that a superabundance of resources favours existence. Quite the contrary. A world superabundant [1] in possibilities automatically produces deformities, vicious types of human life, which may be brought under the general class, the "heir-man," of which the "aristocrat" is only one particular case, the spoiled child another, and the mass-man of our time, more fully, more radically, a third. (It would, moreover, be possible to make more detailed use of this last allusion to the "aristocrat," by showing how many of his characteristic traits, in all times and among all peoples, germinate in the mass-man. For example: his propensity to make out of games and sports the central occupation of his life; the cult of the body— hygienic regime and attention to dress; lack of romance in his dealings with woman; his amusing himself with the "intellectual," while at bottom despising him and at times ordering his flunkeys or his bravoes to chastise him; his preference for living under an absolute author- ity rather than under a regime of free-discussion,[2] etc.)

[1] The increase, and even the abundance, of resources are not to be confused with the excess. In the XIXth Century the facilities of life increase, and this produces the amazing growth—quantita- tive and qualitative—of life that I have noted above. But a moment has come when the civilised world, in relation to the capacity of the average man, has taken on an appearance of superabun- dance, of excess of riches, of superfluity. A single example of this: the security seemingly offered by progress (i.e. the ever-growing increase of vital advantages) demoralised the average man, inspir- ing him with a confidence which is false, vicious, and atrophying.
[2] In this, as in other matters, the English aristocracy seems to be an exception to what we have said. But though the case is an admirable one, it would suffice to indicate in outline the history of England in order to show that this exception proves the rule. Contrary to what is usually said, the English nobility has been the least "superabundant" of Europe, and has lived in more con- stant danger than any other. And because it has always lived in danger, it has succeeded in winning respect for itself—which im- plies that it has ceaselessly remained in the breach. The funda- mental fact is forgotten that England was until well on into the XVIIIth Century the poorest country in Western Europe. It was

I persist then, at the risk of boring the reader, in making the point that this man full of uncivilised tendencies, this newest of the barbarians, is an automatic product of modern civilisation, especially of the form taken by this civilisation in the XIXth Century. He has not burst in on the civilised world from outside like the "great white barbarians" of the Vth Century; neither has he been produced within it by spontaneous, mysterious generation, as Aristotle says of the tadpoles in the pond; he is its natural fruit. One may formulate, as follows, a law confirmed by palaeontology and bio-geography: human life has arisen and progressed only when the resources it could count on were balanced by the problems it met with. This is true, as much in the spiritual order as in the physical. Thus, to refer to a very concrete aspect of corporal existence, I may recall that the human species has flourished in zones of our planet where the hot season is compensated by a season of intense cold. In the tropics the animal-man degenerates, and vice versa, inferior races—the pygmies, for example—have been pushed back towards the tropics by races born after them and superior in the scale of evolution.[1]

The civilisation of the XIXth Century is, then, of such a character that it allows the average man to take his place in a world of superabundance, of which he perceives only the lavishness of the means at his disposal, nothing of the pains involved. He finds himself surrounded by marvellous instruments, healing medicines, watchful governments, comfortable privileges. On the

---

this fact that saved the nobility. Not being abundant in resources, it had very early to enter into commercial and industrial occupations—considered ignoble on the Continent—that is to say, it decided very soon to lead an economic existence creative in character, and not to depend solely on its privileges.

[1] See Olbricht, *Klima und Entwicklung*, 1923.

other hand, he is ignorant how difficult it is to invent those medicines and those instruments and to assure their production in the future; he does not realise how unstable is the organisation of the State and is scarcely conscious to himself of any obligations. This lack of balance falsifies his nature, vitiates it in its very roots, causing him to lose contact with the very substance of life, which is made up of absolute danger, is radically problematic. The form most contradictory to human life that can appear among the human species is the "self-satisfied man." Consequently, when he becomes the predominant type, it is time to raise the alarm and to announce that humanity is threatened with degeneration, that is, with relative death. On this view, the vital level represented by Europe at the present day is superior to the whole of the human past, but if we look to the future, we are made to fear that it will neither preserve the level reached nor attain to a higher one, but rather will recede and fall back upon lower heights.

This, I think, brings out with sufficient clearness the superlative abnormality represented by the "self-satisfied man." He is a man who has entered upon life to do "what he jolly well likes." This, in fact, is the illusion suffered by the *fils de famille*. We know the reason why: in the family circle, everything, even the greatest faults, are in the long run left unpunished. The family circle is relatively artificial, and tolerates many acts which in society, in the world outside, would automatically involve disastrous consequences for their author. But the man of this type thinks that he can behave outside just as he does at home; believes that nothing is fatal, irremediable, irrevocable. That is why he thinks that he can do what he likes.[1] An almighty mistake! "You will go where you are

---

[1] What the home is in relation to society, such on a larger scale is one nation before the assemblage of nations. One of the manifesta-

taken to," as the parrot is told in the Portuguese story. It is not that one *ought* not to do just what one pleases; it is simply that one cannot do other than what each of us *has* to do, *has* to be. The only way out is to refuse to do what has to be done, but this does not set us free to do something else just because it pleases us. In this matter we only possess a negative freedom of will, a *noluntas*. We can quite well turn away from our true destiny, but only to fall a prisoner in the deeper dungeons of our destiny. I cannot make this clear to each of my readers in what concerns his individual destiny as such, because I do not know each of my readers; but it is possible to make it clear in those portions, those facets, of his destiny which are identical with those of others. For example, every present-day European knows, with a certainty much more forcible than that of all his expressed "ideas" and "opinions," that the European of to-day *must* be a liberal. Let us not discuss whether it is this or the other form of liberalism which must be his. I am referring to the fact that the most reactionary of Europeans knows, in the depths of his conscience, that the effort made by Europe in the last century, under the name of liberalism, is, in the last resort, something inevitable, inexorable; something that Western man to-day *is*, whether he likes it or no.

Even though it be proved, with full and incontrovertible evidence, that there is falsity and fatality in all the concrete shapes under which the attempt has been made to realise the categorical imperative of political liberty, inscribed on the destiny of Europe, the final evidence that

---

tions, at once most evident and overwhelming, of the ruling "self-satisfaction" is, as we shall see, the determination taken by some nations to "do what they jolly well please" in the consortium of nations. This, in their ingenuousness, they call "nationalism." I, who detest all false submission to internationalism, find absurd, on the other hand, this passing phase of self-conceit on the part of the least developed of the nations.

in the last century it was right *in substance* still holds good. This final evidence is present equally in the European Communist as in the Fascist, whatever attitudes they may adopt to convince themselves to the contrary. All "know" that beyond all the just criticisms launched against the manifestations of liberalism there remains its unassailable truth, a truth not theoretic, scientific, intellectual, but of an order radically different and more decisive, namely, a truth of destiny. Theoretic truths not only are disputable, but their whole meaning and force lie in their being disputed, they spring from discussion. They live as long as they are discussed, and they are made *exclusively* for discussion. But destiny—what from a vital point of view one has to be or has not to be—is not discussed, it is either accepted or rejected. If we accept it, we are genuine; if not, we are the negation, the falsification of ourselves.[1] Destiny does not consist in what we feel we should like to do; rather is it recognised in its clear features in the consciousness that we *must* do what we do not feel like doing.

Well, then, the "satisfied man" is characterised by his "knowing" that certain things cannot be, and nevertheless, for that very reason, pretending in act and word to be convinced of the opposite. The Fascist will take his stand against political liberty, precisely because he knows that in the long run this can never fail, but is inevitably a part of the very substance of European life, and will be returned to when its presence is truly required, in the hour of grave crisis. For the tonic that keeps the mass-man in form is insincerity, "the joke." All his actions are devoid of the note of inevitability, they are done as the *fils de*

---

[1] Abasement, degradation is simply the manner of life of the man who has refused to be what it is his duty to be. This, his genuine being, none the less does not die; rather is changed into an accusing shadow, a phantom which constantly makes him feel the inferiority of the life he lives compared with the one he ought to live. The debased man survives his self-inflicted death.

famille carries out his escapades. All that haste, in every order of life, to adopt tragic, conclusive, final attitudes is mere appearance. Men play at tragedy because they do not believe in the reality of the tragedy which is actually being staged in the civilised world.

It would be a nice matter if we were forced to accept as the genuine self of an individual, whatever he tried to make us accept as such. If anyone persists in maintaining that he believes two and two make five, and there is no reason for supposing him to be insane, we may be certain that he does not believe it, however much he may shout it out, or even if he allows himself to be killed for maintaining it. A hurricane of farcicality, everywhere and in every form, is at present raging over the lands of Europe. Almost all the positions taken up and proclaimed are false ones. The only efforts that are being made are to escape from our real destiny, to blind ourselves to its evidence, to be deaf to its deep appeal, to avoid facing up to *what has to be*. We are living in comic fashion, all the more comic the more apparently tragic is the mask adopted. The comic exists wherever life has no basis of inevitableness on which a stand is taken without reserves. The mass-man will not plant his foot on the immovably firm ground of his destiny, he prefers a fictitious existence suspended in air. Hence, never as now have we had these lives without substance or root—*déracinés* from their own destiny—which let themselves float on the lightest current. This is the epoch of "currents" and of "letting things slide." Hardly anyone offers any resistance to the superficial whirlwinds that arise in art, in ideas, in politics, or in social usages. Consequently, rhetoric flourishes more than ever. The surrealist thinks he has outstripped the whole of literary history when he has written (here a word that there is no need to write) where others have written "jasmines, swans and fauns." But what he has

really done has been simply to bring to light another form
of rhetoric which hitherto lay hidden in the latrines.

The present situation is made more clear by noting
what, in spite of its peculiar features, it has in common
with past periods. Thus, hardly does Mediterranean civilisation reach its highest point—towards the IIIrd Century
B.C.—when the cynic makes his appearance. Diogenes, in
his mud-covered sandals, tramps over the carpets of Aris-
tippus. The cynic pullulated at every corner, and in the
highest places. This cynic did nothing but *saboter* the
civilisation of the time. He was the nihilist of Hellenism.
He created nothing, he made nothing. His role was to
undo—or rather to attempt to undo, for he did not succeed in his purpose. The cynic, a parasite of civilisation,
lives by denying it, for the very reason that he is convinced that it will not fail. What would become of the
cynic among a savage people where everyone, naturally
and quite seriously, fulfils what the cynic farcically considers to be his personal role? What is your Fascist if he
does not speak ill of liberty, or your surrealist if he does
not blaspheme against art?

None other could be the conduct of this type of man
born into a too well-organised world, of which he perceives only the advantages and not the dangers. His surroundings spoil him, because they are "civilisation," that
is, a home, and the *fils de famille* feels nothing that impels
him to abandon his mood of caprice, nothing which
urges him to listen to outside counsels from those superior
to himself. Still less anything which obliges him to make
contact with the inexorable depths of his own destiny.

12

The Barbarism of
"Specialisation"

MY THESIS was that XIXth-Century civilisation has automatically produced the mass-man. It will be well not to close the general exposition without analysing, in a particular case, the mechanism of that production. In this way, by taking concrete form, the thesis gains in persuasive force.

This civilisation of the XIXth Century, I said, may be summed up in the two great dimensions: liberal democracy and technicism. Let us take for the moment only the latter. Modern technicism springs from the union between capitalism and experimental science. Not all technicism is scientific. That which made the stone axe in the Chelian period was lacking in science, and yet a technique was created. China reached a high degree of technique without in the least suspecting the existence of physics. It is only modern European technique that has a scientific basis, from which it derives its specific character, its possibility of limitless progress. All other techniques—Mesopotamian, Egyptian, Greek, Roman, Oriental—reach up to a point of development beyond which they cannot proceed, and hardly do they reach it when they commence to display a lamentable retrogression.

This marvellous Western technique has made possible the proliferation of the European species. Recall the fact from which this essay took its departure and which, as I said, contains in germ all these present considerations. From the VIth Century to 1800, Europe never succeeds in reaching a population greater than 180 millions. From 1800 to 1914 it rises to more than 460 millions. The jump is unparalleled in our history. There can be no doubt that it is technicism—in combination with liberal democracy—which has engendered mass-man in the quantitative sense of the expression. But these pages have attempted to show that it is also responsible for the existence of mass-man in the qualitative and pejorative sense of the term.

By mass—as I pointed out at the start—is not to be specially understood the workers; it does not indicate a social class, but a kind of man to be found to-day in all social classes, who consequently represents our age, in which he is the predominant, ruling power. We are now about to find abundant evidence for this.

Who is it that exercises social power to-day? Who imposes the forms of his own mind on the period? Without a doubt, the man of the middle class. Which group, within that middle class, is considered the superior, the aristocracy of the present? Without a doubt, the technician: engineer, doctor, financier, teacher, and so on. Who, inside the group of technicians, represents it at its best and purest? Again, without a doubt, the man of science. If an astral personage were to visit Europe to-day and, for the purpose of forming judgment on it, inquire as to the type of man by which it would prefer to be judged, there is no doubt that Europe, pleasantly assured of a favourable judgment, would point to her men of science. Of course, our astral personage would not inquire for exceptional individuals, but would seek the generic type of "man of science," the high-point of European humanity.

And now it turns out that the actual scientific man is the prototype of the mass-man. Not by chance, not through the individual failings of each particular man of science, but because science itself—the root of our civilisation—automatically converts him into mass-man, makes of him a primitive, a modern barbarian. The fact is well known; it has made itself clear over and over again; but only when fitted into its place in the organism of this thesis does it take on its full meaning and its evident seriousness.

Experimental science is initiated towards the end of the XVIth Century (Galileo), it is definitely constituted at the close of the XVIIth (Newton), and it begins to develop in the middle of the XVIIIth. The development of anything is not the same as its constitution; it is subject to different conditions. Thus, the constitution of physics, the collective name of the experimental sciences, rendered necessary an effort towards unification. Such was the work of Newton and other men of his time. But the development of physics introduced a task opposite in character to unification. In order to progress, science demanded specialisation, not in herself, but in men of science. Science is not specialist. If it were, it would *ipso facto* cease to be true. Not even empirical science, taken in its integrity, can be true if separated from mathematics, from logic, from philosophy. But scientific work does, necessarily, require to be specialised.

It would be of great interest, and of greater utility than at first sight appears, to draw up the history of physical and biological sciences, indicating the process of increasing specialisation in the work of investigators. It would then be seen how, generation after generation, the scientist has been gradually restricted and confined into narrower fields of mental occupation. But this is not the important point that such a history would show, but rather the reverse side of the matter: how in each generation the scientist, through having to reduce the sphere of his labour, was progressively losing contact with other branches of science, with that integral interpretation of the universe which is the only thing deserving the names of science, culture, European civilisation.

Specialisation commences precisely at a period which gives to civilised man the title "encyclopaedic." The XIXth Century starts on its course under the direction of beings who lived "encyclopaedically," though their production has already some tinge of specialism. In the following generation, the balance is upset and specialism begins to dislodge integral culture from the individual scientist. When by 1890 a third generation assumes intellectual command in Europe we meet with a type of scientist unparalleled in history. He is one who, out of all that has to be known in order to be a man of judgment, is only acquainted with one science, and even of that one only knows the small corner in which he is an active investigator. He even proclaims it as a virtue that he takes no cognisance of what lies outside the narrow territory specially cultivated by himself, and gives the name of "dilettantism" to any curiosity for the general scheme of knowledge.

What happens is that, enclosed within the narrow limits of his visual field, he does actually succeed in discovering new facts and advancing the progress of the science which he hardly knows, and incidentally the encyclopedia of thought of which he is conscientiously ignorant. How has such a thing been possible, how is it still possible? For it is necessary to insist upon this extraordinary but undeniable fact: experimental science has progressed thanks in great part to the work of men astoundingly mediocre, and even less than mediocre. That is to say, modern science, the root and symbol of our actual civilisation, finds a place for the intellectually commonplace man and allows him to work therein with success. The reason of this lies in what is at the same time the great advantage and the gravest peril of the new science, and of the civilisation directed and represented by it, namely, mechanisation. A fair amount of the things that have to be done in physics or in biology is mechanical work of the mind which can be done by anyone, or almost anyone. For the purpose of innumerable investigations it is possible to divide science into small sections, to enclose oneself in one of these, and to leave out of consideration all the rest. The solidity and exactitude of the methods allow of this temporary but quite real disarticulation of knowledge. The work is done under one of these methods as with a machine, and in order to obtain quite abundant results it is not even necessary to have rigorous notions of their meaning and foundations. In this way the majority of scientists help the general advance of science while shut up in the narrow cell of their laboratory, like the bee in the cell of its hive, or the turnspit in its wheel.

But this creates an extraordinarily strange type of man. The investigator who has discovered a new fact of Nature must necessarily experience a feeling of power and self-assurance. With a certain apparent justice he will look upon himself as "a man who knows." And in fact there is in him a portion of something which, added to many other portions not existing in him, does really constitute knowledge. This is the true inner nature of the specialist, who in the first years of this century has reached the wildest stage of exaggeration. The specialist "knows" very well his own tiny corner of the universe; he is radically ignorant of all the rest.

Here we have a precise example of this strange new man, whom I have attempted to define, from both of his two opposite aspects. I have said that he was a human product unparalleled in history. The specialist serves as a striking concrete example of the species, making clear to us the radical nature of the novelty. For, previously, men could be divided simply into the learned and the ignorant, those more or less the one, and those more or less the other. But your specialist cannot be brought in under either of these two categories. He is not learned, for he is formally ignorant of all that does not enter into his speciality; but neither is he ignorant, because he is "a scientist," and "knows" very well his own tiny portion of the universe. We shall have to say that he is a learned ignoramus, which is a very serious matter, as it implies that he is a person who is ignorant, not in the fashion of the ignorant man, but with all the petulance of one who is learned in his own special line.

And such in fact is the behaviour of the specialist. In politics, in art, in social usages, in the other sciences, he will adopt the attitude of primitive, ignorant man; but he will adopt them forcefully and with self-sufficiency, and will not admit of—this is the paradox—specialists in those matters. By specialising him, civilisation has made him hermetic and self-satisfied within his limitations; but this very inner feeling of dominance and worth will induce him to wish to predominate outside his speciality. The result is that even in this case, representing a maximum of qualification in man—specialisation—and therefore the thing most opposed to the mass-man, the result is that he will behave in almost all spheres of life as does the unqualified, the mass-man.

This is no mere wild statement. Anyone who wishes can observe the stupidity of thought, judgment, and action shown to-day in politics, art, religion, and the general problems of life and the world by the "men of science," and of course, behind them, the doctors, engineers, financiers, teachers, and so on. That state of "not listening," of not submitting to higher courts of appeal which I have repeatedly put forward as characteristic of the mass-man, reaches its height precisely in these partially qualified men. They symbolise, and to a great extent constitute, the actual domination of the masses, and their barbarism is the most immediate cause of European demoralisation. Furthermore, they afford the clearest, most striking example of how the civilisation of the last century, *abandoned to its own devices*, has brought about this rebirth of primitivism and barbarism.

The most immediate result of this *unbalanced* specialisation has been that to-day, when there are more "scientists" than ever, there are much less "cultured" men than, for example, about 1750. And the worst is that with these turnspits of science not even the real progress of science itself is assured. For science needs from time to time, as a necessary regulator of its own advance, a labour of reconstitution, and, as I have said, this demands an effort towards unification, which grows more and more difficult, involving, as it does, ever-vaster regions of the world of knowledge. Newton was able to found his system of physics without knowing much philosophy, but Einstein needed to saturate himself with Kant and Mach before he could reach his own keen synthesis. Kant and Mach—the names are mere symbols of the enormous mass of philosophic and psychological thought which has influenced Einstein—have served to *liberate* the mind of the latter and leave the way open for his innovation. But Einstein is not sufficient. Physics is entering on the gravest crisis of its history, and can only be saved by a new "Encyclopaedia" more systematic than the first.

The specialisation, then, that has made possible the progress of experimental science during a century, is approaching a stage where it can no longer continue its advance unless a new generation undertakes to provide it with a more powerful form of turnspit.

But if the specialist is ignorant of the inner philosophy of the science he cultivates, he is much more radically ignorant of the historical conditions requisite for its continuation; that is to say: how society and the heart of man are to be organised in order that there may continue to be investigators. The decrease in scientific vocations noted in recent years, to which I have alluded, is an anxious symptom for anyone who has a clear idea of what civilisation is, an idea generally lacking to the typical "scientist," the high-point of our present civilisation. He also believes that civilisation *is there* in just the same way as the earth's crust and the forest primeval.

13

The Greatest Danger, the State

IN A RIGHT ordering of public affairs, the mass is that part which does not act of itself. Such is its mission. It has come into the world in order to be directed, influenced, represented, organised—even in order to cease being mass, or at least to aspire to this. But it has not come into the world to do all this by itself. It needs to submit its life to a higher court, formed of the superior minorities. The question as to who are these superior individuals may be discussed *ad libitum*, but that without them, whoever they be, humanity would cease to preserve its essentials is something about which there can be no possible doubt, though Europe spend a century with its head under its wing, ostrich-fashion, trying if she can to avoid seeing such a plain truth. For we are not dealing with an opinion based on facts more or less frequent and probable, but on a law of social "physics," much more immovable than the laws of Newton's physics. The day when a genuine philosophy [1] once more holds sway in

[1] For philosophy to rule, it is not necessary that philosophers be the rulers—as Plato at first wished—nor even for rulers to be philosophers—as was his later, more modest, wish. Both these things are, strictly speaking, most fatal. For philosophy to rule, it is sufficient for it to exist; that is to say, for the philosophers to be philosophers. For nearly a century past, philosophers have been everything but that—politicians, pedagogues, men of letters, and men of science.

Europe—it is the one thing that can save her—that day she will once again realise that man, whether he like it or no, is a being forced by his nature to seek some higher authority. If he succeeds in finding it of himself, he is a superior man; if not, he is a mass-man and must receive it from his superiors.

For the mass to claim the right to act of itself is then a rebellion against its own destiny, and because that is what it is doing at present, I speak of the rebellion of the masses. For, after all, the one thing that can substantially and truthfully be called rebellion is that which consists in not accepting one's own destiny, in rebelling against one's self. The rebellion of the archangel Lucifer would not have been less if, instead of striving to be God —which was not his destiny—he had striven to be the lowest of the angels—equally not his destiny. (If Lucifer had been a Russian, like Tolstoi, he would perhaps have preferred this latter form of rebellion, none the less against God than the other more famous one.)

When the mass acts on its own, it does so only in one way, for it has no other: it lynches. It is not altogether by chance that lynch law comes from America, for America is, in a fashion, the paradise of the masses. And it will cause less surprise, nowadays, when the masses triumph, that violence should triumph and be made the one *ratio*, the one doctrine. It is now some time since I called attention to this advance of violence as a normal condition.[1] To-day it has reached its full development, and this is a good symptom, because it means that automatically the descent is about to begin. To-day violence is the rhetoric of the period, the empty rhetorician has made it his own. When a reality of human existence has completed its historic course, has been shipwrecked and lies dead, the waves throw it up on the shores of rhetoric,

[1] Vide *España Invertebrada*, 1912.

where the corpse remains for a long time. Rhetoric is the cemetery of human realities, or at any rate a Home for the Aged. The reality itself is survived by its name, which, though only a word, is after all at least a word and preserves something of its magic power.

But though it is not impossible that the prestige of violence as a cynically established rule has entered on its decline, we shall still continue under that rule, though in another form. I refer to the gravest danger now threatening European civilisation. Like all other dangers that threaten it, this one is born of civilisation itself. More than that, it constitutes one of its glories: it is the State as we know it to-day. We are confronted with a replica of what we said in the previous chapter about science: the fertility of its principles brings about a fabulous progress, but this inevitably imposes specialisation, and specialisation threatens to strangle science.

The same thing is happening with the State. Call to mind what the State was at the end of the XVIIIth Century in all European nations. Quite a small affair! Early capitalism and its industrial organisation, in which the new, rationalised technique triumphs for the first time, had brought about a commencement of increase in society. A new social class appeared, greater in numbers and power than the pre-existing: the middle class. This astute middle class possessed one thing, above and before all: talent, practical talent. It knew how to organise and discipline, how to give continuity and consistency to its efforts. In the midst of it, as in an ocean, the "ship of State" sailed its hazardous course. The ship of State is a metaphor re-invented by the bourgeoisie, which felt itself oceanic, omnipotent, pregnant with storms. That ship was, as we said, a very small affair: it had hardly any soldiers, bureaucrats, or money. It had been built in the Middle Ages by a class of men very different from the bourgeois—the nobles, a class admirable for their courage, their gifts of leadership, their sense of responsibility. Without them the nations of Europe would not now be in existence. But with all those virtues of the heart, the nobles were, and always have been, lacking in virtues of the head. Of limited intelligence, sentimental, instinctive, intuitive—in a word, "irrational." Hence they were unable to develop any technique, a thing which demands rationalisation. They did not invent gunpowder. Incapable of inventing new arms, they allowed the bourgeois, who got it from the East or somewhere else, to utilise gunpowder and automatically to win the battle against the warrior noble, the "caballero," stupidly covered in iron so that he could hardly move in the fight, and who had never imagined that the eternal secret of warfare consists not so much in the methods of defence as in those of attack, a secret which was to be rediscovered by Napoleon.[1]

As the State is a matter of technique—of public order and administration—the "ancien régime" reaches the end of the XVIIIth Century with a very weak State, harassed on all sides by a widespread social revolt. The disproportion between State power and social power at this time

[1] We owe to Ranke this simple picture of the great historic change by which for the supremacy of the nobles is substituted the predominance of the bourgeois; but of course its symbolic geometric outlines require no little filling-in in order to be completely true. Gunpowder was known from time immemorial. The invention by which a tube was charged with it was due to someone in Lombardy. Even then it was not efficacious until the invention of the cast cannon-ball. The "nobles" used firearms to a small extent, but they were too dear for them. It was only the bourgeois armies, with their better economic organisation, that could employ them on a large scale. It remains, however, literally true that the nobles, represented by the medieval type of army of the Burgundians, were definitely defeated by the new army, not professional but bourgeois, formed by the Swiss. Their primary force lay in the new discipline and the new rationalisation of tactics.

is such that, comparing the situation then with that of the time of Charlemagne, the XVIIIth-Century State appears degenerate. The Carolingian State was of course much less powerful than the State of Louis XVI, but, on the other hand, the society surrounding it was entirely lacking in strength.[1] The enormous disproportion between social strength and the strength of public power made possible the Revolution, the revolutions—up to 1848.

But with the Revolution the middle class took possession of public power and applied their undeniable qualities to the State, and in little more than a generation created a powerful State, which brought revolutions to an end. Since 1848, that is to say, since the beginning of the second generation of bourgeois governments, there have been no genuine revolutions in Europe. Not assuredly because there were no motives for them, but because there were no means. Public power was brought to the level of social power. *Good-bye for ever to Revolutions!* The only thing now possible in Europe is their opposite: the *coup d'état*. Everything which in following years tried to look like a revolution was only a *coup d'état* in disguise.

In our days the State has come to be a formidable machine which works in marvellous fashion; of wonderful efficiency by reason of the quantity and precision of its

---

[1] It would be worth while insisting on this point and making clear that the epoch of absolute monarchies in Europe has coincided with very weak States. How is this to be explained? Why, if the State was all-powerful, "absolute," did it not make itself stronger? One of the causes is that indicated, the incapacity—technical, organising, bureaucratic—of the aristocracies of blood. But this is not enough. Besides that, it also happened that the absolute State and those aristocracies *did not want to aggrandise the State at the expense of society in general.* Contrary to the common belief, the absolute State instinctively respects society much more than our democratic State, which is more intelligent but has less sense of historic responsibility.

means. Once it is set up in the midst of society, it is
enough to touch a button for its enormous levers to start
working and exercise their overwhelming power on any
portion whatever of the social framework.

The contemporary State is the easiest seen and best-
known product of civilisation. And it is an interesting
revelation when one takes note of the attitude that mass-
man adopts before it. He sees it, admires it, knows that
there it is, safeguarding his existence; but he is not conscious of the fact that it is a human creation invented by
certain men and upheld by certain virtues and fundamental qualities which the men of yesterday had and
which may vanish into air to-morrow. Furthermore, the
mass-man sees in the State an anonymous power, and
feeling himself, like it, anonymous, he believes that the
State is something of his own. Suppose that in the public
life of a country some difficulty, conflict, or problem presents itself, the mass-man will tend to demand that the
State intervene immediately and undertake a solution directly with its immense and unassailable resources.

This is the gravest danger that to-day threatens civilisation: State intervention; the absorption of all spontaneous social effort by the State, that is to say, of spontaneous historical action, which in the long run sustains,
nourishes, and impels human destinies. When the mass
suffers any ill-fortune or simply feels some strong appetite, its great temptation is that permanent, sure possibility
of obtaining everything—without effort, struggle, doubt,
or risk—merely by touching a button and setting the
mighty machine in motion. The mass says to itself, "*L'État,
c'est moi*," which is a complete mistake. The State is the
mass only in the sense in which it can be said of two
men that they are identical because neither of them is
named John. The contemporary State and the mass coincide only in being anonymous. But the mass-man does in

fact believe that he is the State, and he will tend more and more to set its machinery working on whatsoever pretext, to crush beneath it any creative minority which disturbs it—disturbs it in any order of things: in politics, in ideas, in industry.

The result of this tendency will be fatal. Spontaneous social action will be broken up over and over again by State intervention; no new seed will be able to fructify. Society will have to live *for* the State, man *for* the governmental machine. And as, after all, it is only a machine whose existence and maintenance depend on the vital supports around it, the State, after sucking out the very marrow of society, will be left bloodless, a skeleton, dead with that rusty death of machinery, more gruesome than the death of a living organism.

Such was the lamentable fate of ancient civilisation. No doubt the imperial State created by the Julii and the Claudii was an admirable machine, incomparably superior as a mere structure to the old republican State of the patrician families. But, by a curious coincidence, hardly had it reached full development when the social body began to decay.

Already in the times of the Antonines (IInd Century), the State overbears society with its anti-vital supremacy. Society begins to be enslaved, to be unable to live except *in the service of the State*. The whole of life is bureaucratised. What results? The bureaucratisation of life brings about its absolute decay in all orders. Wealth diminishes, births are few. Then the State, in order to attend to its own needs, forces on still more the bureaucratisation of human existence. This bureaucratisation to the second power is the militarisation of society. The State's most urgent need is its apparatus of war, its army. Before all the State is the producer of security (that security, be it remembered, of which the mass-man is born).

Hence, above all, an army. The Severi, of African origin, militarise the world. Vain task! Misery increases, women are every day less fruitful, even soldiers are lacking. After the time of the Severi, the army has to be recruited from foreigners.

Is the paradoxical, tragic process of Statism now realised? Society, that it may live better, creates the State as an instrument. Then the State gets the upper hand and society has to begin to live for the State.[1] But for all that the State is still composed of the members of that society. But soon these do not suffice to support it, and it has to call in foreigners: first Dalmatians, then Germans. These foreigners take possession of the State, and the rest of society, the former populace, has to live as their slaves— slaves of people with whom they have nothing in common. This is what State intervention leads to: the people are converted into fuel to feed the mere machine which is the State. The skeleton eats up the flesh around it. The scaffolding becomes the owner and tenant of the house.

When this is realised, it rather confounds one to hear Mussolini heralding as an astounding discovery just made in Italy, the formula: "All for the State; nothing outside the State; nothing against the State." This alone would suffice to reveal in Fascism a typical movement of mass-men. Mussolini found a State admirably built up—not by him, but precisely by the ideas and the forces he is combating: by liberal democracy. He confines himself to using it ruthlessly, and, without entering now into a detailed examination of his work, it is indisputable that the results obtained up to the present cannot be compared with those obtained in political and administrative working by the liberal State. If he has succeeded in anything,

---

[1] Recall the last words of Septimus Severus to his sons: "Remain united, pay the soldiers, and take no heed of the rest."

it is so minute, so little visible, so lacking in substance as with difficulty to compensate for the accumulation of the abnormal powers which enable him to make use of that machine to its full extent.

Statism is the higher form taken by violence and direct action when these are set up as standards. Through and by means of the State, the anonymous machine, the masses act for themselves. The nations of Europe have before them a period of great difficulties in their internal life, supremely arduous problems of law, economics, and public order. Can we help feeling that under the rule of the masses the State will endeavour to crush the independence of the individual and the group, and thus definitely spoil the harvest of the future?

A concrete example of this mechanism is found in one of the most alarming phenomena of the last thirty years: the enormous increase in the police force of all countries. The increase of population has inevitably rendered it necessary. However accustomed we may be to it, the terrible paradox should not escape our minds that the population of a great modern city, in order to move about peaceably and attend to its business, necessarily requires a police force to regulate the circulation. But it is foolishness for the party of "law and order" to imagine that these "forces of public authority" created to preserve order are always going to be content to preserve the order that that party desires. Inevitably they will end by themselves defining and deciding on the order they are going to impose—which, naturally, will be that which suits them best.

It might be well to take advantage of our touching on this matter to observe the different reaction to a public need manifested by different types of society. When, about 1800, the new industry began to create a type of man—the industrial worker—more criminally inclined than traditional types, France hastened to create a numerous police force. Towards 1810 there occurs in England, for the same reasons, an increase in criminality, and the English suddenly realise that they have no police. The Conservatives are in power. What will they do? Will they establish a police force? Nothing of the kind. They prefer to put up with crime, as well as they can. "People are content to let disorder alone, considering it the price they pay for liberty." "In Paris," writes John William Ward, "they have an admirable police force, but they pay dear for its advantages. I prefer to see, every three or four years, half a dozen people getting their throats cut in the Ratcliffe Road, than to have to submit to domiciliary visits, to spying, and to all the machinations of Fouché." [1] Here we have two opposite ideas of the State. The Englishman demands that the State should have limits set to it.

[1] *Vide* Elie Halévy, *Histoire du peuple anglais au XIX siècle*, Vol. I, p. 40 (1912).

14

Who Rules in the World?

EUROPEAN civilisation, I have repeated more than once, has automatically brought about the rebellion of the masses. From one view-point this fact presents a most favourable aspect, as we have noted: the rebellion of the masses is one and the same thing as the fabulous increase that human existence has experienced in our times. But the reverse side of the same phenomenon is fearsome; it is none other than the radical demoralisation of humanity. Let us now consider this last from new view-points.

1

The substance or character of a new historical period is the resultant of internal variations—of man and his spirit; or of external variations—formal, and as it were mechanical. Amongst these last, the most important, almost without a doubt, is the displacement of power. But this brings with it a displacement of the spirit.

Consequently, when we set about examining a period with a view to understanding it, one of our first questions ought to be: who is governing in the world at the time? It may happen that at the time humanity is scattered in different groups without any communication, forming interior, independent worlds. In the days of Miltiades, the Mediterranean world was unaware of the existence of the Far-Eastern world. In such cases we shall have to refer our question, "Who rules in the world?" to each individual group. But from the XVIth Century, humanity has entered on a vast unifying process, which in our days has reached its furthest limits. There is now no portion of humanity living apart—no islands of human existence. Consequently, from that century on, it may be said that whoever rules the world does, in fact, exercise authoritative influence over the whole of it. Such has been the part played by the homogeneous group formed by European peoples during the last three centuries. Europe was the ruler, and under its unity of command the world lived in unitary fashion, or at least was progressively unified. This fashion of existence is generally styled the Modern Age, a colourless, inexpressive name, under which lies hidden this reality: the epoch of European hegemony.

By "rule" we are not here to understand primarily the exercise of material power, of physical coercion. We are here trying to avoid foolish notions, at least the more gross and evident ones. This stable, normal relation amongst men which is known as "rule" *never rests on force;* on the contrary, it is because a man or group of men exercise command that they have at their disposition that social apparatus or machinery known as "force." The cases in which at first sight force seems to be the basis of command, are revealed on a closer inspection as the best example to prove our thesis. Napoleon led an aggressive force against Spain, maintained his aggression for a time, but, properly speaking, never ruled in Spain for a single day. And that, although he had the force, and precisely because he had it. It is necessary to distinguish between a process of aggression and a state of rule. Rule is the normal exercise of authority, and is always based on public opinion, to-day as a thousand years ago, amongst the English as amongst the bushmen. Never has anyone ruled on this earth by basing his rule essentially on any other thing than public opinion.

It may be thought that the sovereignty of public opinion was an invention of the lawyer Danton, in 1789, or of Saint Thomas Aquinas in the XIIIth Century. The notion of that sovereignty may have been discovered in one place or another, at one time or another, but the fact that public opinion is the basic force which produces the phenomenon of rule in human societies is as old, and as lasting, as mankind. In Newton's physics gravitation is the force which produces movement. And the law of public opinion is the universal law of gravitation in political history. Without it the science of history would be impossible. Hence Hume's acute suggestion that the theme of history consists in demonstrating how the sovereignty of public opinion, far from being a Utopian aspiration, is what has actually happened everywhere and always in human societies. Even the man who attempts to rule with janissaries depends on their opinion and the opinion which the rest of the inhabitants have of them.

The truth is that there is no ruling with janissaries. As Talleyrand said to Napoleon: "You can do everything with bayonets, Sire, except sit on them." And to rule is not the gesture of snatching at power, but the tranquil exercise of it. In a word, to rule is to sit down, be it on the throne, curule chair, front bench, or bishop's seat. Contrary to the unsophisticated suggestions of melodrama, to rule is not so much a question of the heavy hand as of the firm seat. The State is, in fine, the state of opinion, a position of equilibrium.

What happens is that at times public opinion is nonexistent. A society divided into discordant groups, with their forces of opinion cancelling one another out, leaves no room for a ruling power to be constituted. And as "nature abhors a vacuum" the empty space left by the absence of public opinion is filled by brute force. At the most, then, the latter presents itself as a substitute for the former. Consequently, if we wish to express the law of public opinion as the law of historical gravitation, we shall take into consideration those cases where it is absent, and we then arrive at a formula which is the well-known, venerable, forthright commonplace: there can be no rule in opposition to public opinion.

This enables us to realise that rule signifies the predominance of an opinion, and therefore of a spirit; that rule is, when all is said and done, nothing else but a spiritual power. This is confirmed with precision by the facts of history. All primitive rule has a "sacred" character, for it is based on religion and religion is the first form under which appears what is afterwards to be spirit, idea, opinion; in a word, the immaterial and ultraphysical. In the Middle Ages the same phenomenon is reproduced on a larger scale. The first State or public authority formed in Europe is the Church, with its specific, well-defined character of "the spiritual power." From the Church the political power learns that it, too, in its origin, is a spiritual authority, the prevalence of certain ideas, and there is created the *Holy* Roman Empire. Thus arises the struggle between two powers, which, having no differentiation in substance (as they are both spirit), reach an agreement by which each limits itself to a time-category; the temporal and the eternal. Temporal power and religious power are equally spiritual, but the one is the spirit of time, public opinion, mundane and fluctuating, whilst the other is the spirit of eternity, the opinion of God, God's view of man and his destiny. It comes to the same thing then to say: At a given period, such a man, such a people, or such a homogeneous group of peoples, are in command, as to say: At this given period there predominates in the world such a system of opinions —ideas, preferences, aspirations, purposes.

How is this predominance to be understood? The majority of men have no opinions, and these have to be

pumped into them from outside, like lubricants into machinery. Hence it is necessary that some mind or other
should hold and exercise authority, so that the people
without opinions—the majority—can start having opinions. For without these, the common life of humanity
would be chaos, a historic void, lacking in any organic
structure. Consequently, without a spiritual power, *without someone to command,* and in proportion as this is
lacking, chaos reigns over mankind. And similarly, all
displacement of power, every change of authority, implies a change of opinions, and therefore nothing less than
a change of historical gravitation. Let us go back again
to where we started from. For several centuries the world
has been ruled by Europe, a conglomerate of peoples
akin in spirit. In the Middle Ages there was no such rule
in temporal matters. So it has happened in all the middle
ages of history. That is why they represent a relative
chaos, relative barbarism, a deficit of public opinion.
They are times in which men love, hate, desire, detest;
all this without limit; but, on the other hand, there is
no opinion. Such epochs are not without their charm.
But in the great epochs, what mankind lives by is opinion, and therefore, order rules. On the further side of the
Middle Ages we also find a period in which, as in the
Modern Age, there is someone in command, though only
over a limited portion of the world: Rome, the great
director. It was she who set up order in the Mediterranean and its borders.

In these post-war times the word is beginning to go
round that Europe no longer rules in the world. Is the
full gravity of this diagnosis realised? By it there is
announced a displacement of power. In what direction?
Who is going to succeed Europe in ruling over the world?
But is it so sure that anyone is going to succeed her?
And if no one, what then is going to happen?

2

It is true, of course, that at any moment, and therefore
actually, an infinity of things is happening in the world.
Any attempt, then, to say what is happening in the
world to-day must be taken as being conscious of its own
irony. But for the very reason that we are unable to have
directly complete knowledge of reality, there is nothing
for us but arbitrarily to construct a reality, to suppose
that things are happening after a certain fashion. This
provides us with an outline, a concept or framework
of concepts. With this, as through a "sight," we then look
at the actual reality, and it is only then that we obtain
an approximate vision of it. It is in this that scientific
method consists. Nay, more, in this consists all use of
the intellect. When we see our friend coming up the
garden path, and we say: "Here's Peter," we are com-
miting, deliberately, ironically, an error. For Peter implies for us a complex of ways of behaviour, physical and
moral—what we call "character"—and the plain truth
is that, at times, our friend Peter is not in the least like
the concept "our friend Peter."

Every concept, the simplest and the most technical,
is framed in its own irony as the geometrically cut dia-
mond is held in its setting of gold. The concept tells us
quite seriously: "This thing is A, that thing is B." But
the seriousness is that of the man who is playing a joke
on you, the unstable seriousness of one who is swallowing a laugh, which will burst out if he does not keep his
lips tight-closed. It knows very well that this thing is
not just merely A, or that thing just merely B. What
the concept really thinks is a little bit different from what
it says, and herein the irony lies. What it really thinks
is this: I know that, strictly speaking, this thing is not
A, nor that thing B; but by taking them as A and B, I

come to an understanding with myself for the purposes of my practical attitude towards both of these things. This theory of rational knowledge would have displeased a Greek. For the Greek believed that he had discovered in the reason, in the concept, reality itself. We, on the contrary, believe that the concept is one of man's household utensils, which he needs and uses in order to make clear his own position in the midst of the infinite and very problematic reality which is his life. Life is a struggle with things to maintain itself among them. Concepts are the strategic plan we form in answer to the attack. Hence, if we penetrate to the true inwardness of a concept, we find that it tells us nothing of the thing itself, but only sums up what one can do with it, or what it can do to one. This opinion, according to which the content of a concept is always vital, is always a possible activity or passivity, has not been maintained, as far as I know, by anyone before now, but it seems to me to be the inevitable outcome of the philosophical processes initiated by Kant. Hence, if by its light, we examine the whole past of philosophy up to the time of Kant, it will seem to us that, *at bottom*, all philosophers have said the same thing. Well, then, every philosophical discovery is nothing else than an uncovering, a bringing to the surface, of what was lying in the depths.

But this is an inordinate introduction to what I am going to say; something quite foreign to philosophical problems. I was simply going to say that what is actually happening in the world of history is this and this alone: for three centuries Europe has been the ruler in the world, and now Europe is no longer sure that she is, or will continue to be, the ruler. To reduce to such a simple formula the historic reality of the present time is doubtless, at the best, an exaggeration, and hence the need I was in of recalling that to think is, whether you want or no, to exaggerate. If you prefer not to exaggerate, you must remain silent; or, rather, you must paralyse your intellect and find some way of becoming an idiot.

I believe, then, that this is what is happening in the world at present, and that all the rest is mere consequence, condition, symptom, or incident of the first. I have not said that Europe has ceased to rule, but that in these times, Europe feels grave doubts as to whether she does rule or not, as to whether she will rule to-morrow. Corresponding to this, there is in the other peoples of the earth a related state of mind, a doubt as to whether they are at present ruled by anyone. They also are not sure of it.

There has been a lot of talk in recent years about the decadence of Europe. I would ask people not to be so simple-minded as to think of Spengler immediately the decadence of Europe or of the West is mentioned. Before his book appeared, everyone was talking of this matter, and as is well known, the success of his book was due to the fact that the suspicion was already existing in people's minds, in ways and for reasons of the most heterogeneous.

There has been so much talk of the decadence of Europe, that many have come to take it for a fact. Not that they believe in it seriously and on proof, but that they have grown used to take it as true, though they cannot honestly recall having convinced themselves decidedly in the matter at any fixed time. Waldo Frank's recent book *The Rediscovery of America* is based entirely on the supposition that Europe is at its last gasp. And yet, Frank neither analyses nor discusses, nor submits to question this enormous fact, which is to serve him as a formidable premise. Without further investigation, he starts from it as from something incontrovertible. And this ingenuousness at the very start is sufficient to make me think that Frank is not convinced of the decadence of Europe; far from it, he has never set himself the problem. He takes it as he would take a tram. Commonplaces are the tramways of intellectual transportation. And as he does, so do many others. Above all, it is done by nations, whole nations.

The world at the present day is behaving in a way which is a very model of childishness. In school, when someone gives the word that the master has left the class, the mob of youngsters breaks loose, kicks up its heels, and goes wild. Each of them experiences the delights of escaping the pressure imposed by the master's presence, of throwing off the yoke of rule, of feeling himself the master of his fate. But as, once the plan which directed their occupations and tasks is suspended, the youthful mob has no formal occupation of its own, no task with a meaning, a continuity, and a purpose, it follows that it can only do one thing—stand on its head. The frivolous spectacle offered by the smaller nations to-day is deplorable. Because it is said that Europe is in decadence and has given over ruling, every tuppeny-ha'penny nation starts skipping, gesticulating, standing on its head or else struts around giving itself airs of a grown-up person who is the ruler of his own destinies. Hence the vibrionic panorama of "nationalisms" that meets our view everywhere.

In previous chapters I attempted to put in his classification a new type of man who to-day predominates in the world: I called him the mass-man, and I observed that his main characteristic lies in that, feeling himself "common," he proclaims the right to be common, and refuses to accept any order superior to himself. It was only natural that if this mentality is predominant in every people, it should be manifest also when we consider the nations as a group. There are then also relatively mass-peoples determined on rebelling against the great creative peoples, the minority of human stocks which have organised history. It is really comic to see how this or the other puny republic, from its out-of-the-way corner, stands up on tip-toe, starts rebuking Europe, and declares that she has lost her place in universal history.

What is the result? Europe had created a system of standards whose efficacy and productiveness the centuries have proved. Those standards are not the best possible; far from it. But they are, without a doubt, definite standards as long as no others exist or are visualised. Before supplanting them, it is essential to produce others. Now, the mass-peoples have decided to consider as bankrupt that system of standards which European civilisation implies, but as they are incapable of creating others, they do not know what to do, and to pass the time they kick up their heels and stand on their heads. Such is the first consequence which follows when there ceases to be in the world anyone who rules; the rest, when they break into rebellion, are left without a task to perform, without a programme of life.

3

The gypsy in the story went to confession, but the cautious priest asked him if he knew the commandments of the law of God. To which the gypsy replied: "Well, Father, it's this way: I *was* going to learn them, but I heard talk that they were going to do away with them."

Is not this the situation in the world at present? The rumour is running round that the commandments of the law of Europe are no longer in force, and in view of this, men and peoples are taking the opportunity of living without imperatives. For the European were the only ones that existed. It is not a question—as has happened

previously—of new standards springing up to displace
the old, or of a new fervour absorbing in its youthful
vigour the old enthusiasms of diminishing temperature.
That would be the natural procedure. Furthermore, the
old is proved to be old not because it is itself falling into
senility, but because it has against it a new principle
which, by the fact of being new, renders old the pre-
existing. If we had no children, we should not be old, or
should take much longer to get old. The same happens
with machines. A motor-car ten years old seems older
than a locomotive of twenty years ago, simply because
the inventions of motor production have followed one
another with greater rapidity. This decadence, which has
its source in the rising-up of fresh youth, is a symptom
of health.

But what is happening at present in Europe is something unhealthy and unusual. The European commandments have lost their force, though there is no sign of
any others on the horizon. Europe—we are told—is ceasing to rule, and no one sees who is going to take her
place. By Europe we understand primarily and properly
the trinity of France, England, Germany. It is in the portion of the globe occupied by these that there has ma-
tured that mode of human existence in accordance with
which the world has been organized. If, as is now announced, these three peoples are in decadence, and their
programme of life has lost its validity, it is not strange
that the world is becoming demoralised.

And such is the simple truth. The whole world—nations and individuals—is demoralised. For a time this
demoralisation rather amuses people, and even causes
a vague illusion. The lower ranks think that a weight has
been lifted off them. Decalogues retain from the time
they were written on stone or bronze their character of
heaviness. The etymology of command conveys the no-

tion of putting a load into someone's hands. He who commands cannot help being a bore. Lower ranks the world over are tired of being ordered and commanded, and with holiday air take advantage of a period freed from burdensome imperatives. But the holiday does not last long. Without commandments, obliging us to live after a certain fashion, our existence is that of the "unemployed." This is the terrible spiritual situation in which the best youth of the world finds itself to-day. By dint of feeling itself free, exempt from restrictions, it feels itself empty. An "unemployed" existence is a worse negation of life than death itself. Because to live means to have something definite to do—a mission to fulfil—and in the measure in which we avoid setting our life to something, we make it empty. Before long there will be heard throughout the planet a formidable cry, rising like the howling of innumerable dogs to the stars, asking for someone or something to take command, to impose an occupation, a duty. This for those people who, with the thoughtlessness of children, announce to us that Europe is no longer in command. To command is to give people something to do, to fit them into their destiny, to prevent their wandering aimlessly about in an empty, desolate existence.

It would not matter if Europe ceased to command, provided there were someone able to take her place. But there is not the faintest sign of one. New York and Moscow represent nothing new, relatively to Europe. They are both of them two sections of the European order of things, which, by dissociating from the rest, have lost their meaning. In sober truth, one is afraid to talk of New York and Moscow, because one does not know what they really are; the only thing one knows is that the decisive word has not yet been said about either of them. But even without full knowledge of what they are, one can arrive at sufficient to understand their generic character. And, in fact, both of them fit in perfectly with what I have sometimes called "phenomena of historical camouflage." Of its nature, camouflage is a reality which is not what it seems. Its appearance, instead of declaring, conceals its substance. Hence the majority of people are deceived. The deception can only be avoided by one who knows beforehand, and in general, that there is such a thing as camouflage. It is the same as with the mirage. The concept we have of the phenomenon corrects our vision.

In every instance of historical camouflage we have two realities superimposed; one genuine and substantial, underneath; the other apparent and accidental, on the surface. So, in Moscow, there is a screen of European ideas —Marxism—thought out in Europe in view of European realities and problems. Behind it there is a people, not merely ethnically distinct from the European, but what is much more important, of a different age to ours. A people still in process of fermentation; that is to say, a child-people. That Marxism should triumph in Russia, where there is no industry, would be the greatest contradiction that Marxism could undergo. But there is no such contradiction, for there is no such triumph. Russia is Marxist more or less as the Germans of the Holy Roman Empire were Romans. New peoples have no ideas. When they grow up in an atmosphere in which an old civilisation exists, or has existed, they disguise themselves in the ideas which it offers to them. Here is the camouflage and the reason for it. As I have observed on other occasions, it is forgotten that there are two main types of evolution for a people. There is the people which is born into a "world" empty of all civilisation, for example the Egyptians or the Chinese. In such a people everything is autochthonous, and their acts have a clear direct sense of their own. But there are other peoples who spring up and develop in a situation already occupied by a civilisation of long history. So Rome, which grows up by the Mediterranean, whose waters were impregnated with Graeco-Oriental culture. Hence half the "gestures" of the Romans are not their own, they have been learnt. And the "gesture" which has been learnt, accepted, has always a double aspect, its real meaning is oblique, not direct. The man who performs an act which he has learnt—speaks a foreign word, for example—carries out beneath it an act of his own, genuine; he translates the foreign term to his own language. Hence, in order to penetrate camouflage an oblique glance is required, the glance of one who is translating a text with the dictionary by his side. I am waiting for the book in which Stalin's Marxism will appear translated into Russian history. For it is this which is Russia's strength, what it has of Russian, not what it has of Communist. Goodness knows what it will be like! The only thing one can assert is that Russia will require centuries before she can aspire to command. Because she is still lacking in commandments she has been obliged to feign adherence to the European principles of Marx. As she has abundant youth, that fiction is enough for her. Youth does not require reasons for living, it only needs pretexts. Something very similar is happening with New York. It is again an error to attribute its actual strength to the commandments it obeys. In the last resort these are reduced to one—technicism. How strange! Another European invention, not an American. Technicism is invented by Europe during the XVIIIth and XIXth Centuries. Again how strange! The very centuries in which America is coming into existence. And we are told quite seriously that the essence of America is its practical and technicist conception of life. Instead of being told that America is, as all colonies are, a rejuvenescence of old races, in particular of Europe. For different reasons to those in the case of Russia, the United States also affords an example of that specific historic reality which we call "a new people." This is looked upon as a mere phrase, when in reality it is a fact as precise as that of youth in man. America is strong by reason of its youth, which has put itself at the service of the modern commandment of technicism, just as it might have put itself at the service of Buddhism, if that were the order of the day. But while acting thus, America is only starting its history. It is only now that its trials, its dissensions, its conflicts, are beginning. It has yet to be many things; amongst others, some things quite opposed to the technical and the practical. America is younger than Russia. I have always maintained, though in fear of exaggeration, that it is a primitive people camouflaged behind the latest inventions.[1] And now Waldo Frank, in his *Rediscovery of America*, declares this openly. America has not yet suffered; it is an illusion to think that it can possess the virtues of command.

Anyone who wishes to escape from the pessimistic conclusion that nobody is going to be in command, and that therefore the historic world is returning into chaos, will have to fall back to the point we started from, and ask himself seriously: Is it as certain as people say that Europe is in decadence; that it is resigning its command; abdicating? May not this apparent decadence be a beneficial crisis which will enable Europe to be really, literally Europe. The evident decadence of the *nations* of Europe, was not this *a priori* necessary if there was to be one day possible a United States of Europe, the plurality of Europe substituted by its formal unity?

[1] See *El Espectador* (VII. *Hegel y America*).

4

The function of commanding and obeying is the decisive one in every society. As long as there is any doubt as to who commands and who obeys, all the rest will be imperfect and ineffective. Even the very consciences of men, apart from special exceptions, will be disturbed and falsified. If man were a solitary being, finding himself only on occasion thrown into association with others, he might come out intact from such disturbances, brought about by the displacements and crises of the ruling Power. But as he is social in his most intimate texture, his personal character is transformed by changes which strictly speaking only immediately affect the collectivity. Hence it is, that if an individual be taken apart and analysed, it is possible without further data to deduce how his country's conscience is organised in the matter of command and obedience.

It would be interesting and even useful to submit to this test the individual character of the average Spaniard. However, the operation would be an unpleasant one, and though useful, depressing, so I avoid it. But it would make clear the enormous dose of personal demoralisation, of degradation, which is produced in the average man of our country by the fact that Spain is a nation which has lived for centuries with a false conscience in the matter of commanding and obeying. This degradation is nothing else than the acceptance, as a normal, constituted condition, of an irregularity, of something which, though accepted, is still regarded as not right. As it is impossible to change into healthy normality what is of its essence unhealthy and abnormal, the individual decides to adapt himself to the thing that is wrong, making himself a part of the crime or irregularity. It is a mechanism similar to that indicated by the popular saying, "One lie makes a hundred." All countries have passed through periods when someone who should not rule has made the attempt to rule over them, but a strong instinct forced them at once to concentrate their energies and to crush that irregular claim to exercise power. They rejected the passing irregularity and thus reconstituted their morale as a people. But the Spaniard has done just the opposite; instead of resisting a form of authority which his innermost conscience repudiated, he has preferred to falsify all the rest of his being in order to bring it into line with that initial unreality. As long as this continues in our country it is vain to hope for anything from the men of our race. There can be no elastic vigour for the difficult task of retaining a worthy position in history in a society whose State, whose authority, is of its very nature a fraud.

There is, then, nothing strange in the fact that a slight doubt, a simple hesitation as to who rules in the world, should be sufficient to bring about a commencement of demoralisation in everyone, both in his public and his private life.

Human life, by its very nature, has to be dedicated to something, an enterprise glorious or humble, a destiny illustrious or trivial. We are faced with a condition, strange but inexorable, involved in our very existence. On the one hand, to live is something which each one does of himself and for himself. On the other hand, if that life of mine, which only concerns myself, is not directed by me towards something, it will be disjointed, lacking in tension and in "form." In these years we are witnessing the gigantic spectacle of innumerable human lives wandering about lost in their own labyrinths, through not having anything to which to give themselves. All imperatives, all commands, are in a state of suspension. The situation might seem to be an ideal one, since every existence is left entirely free to do just as it pleases—to look after itself. The same with every nation. Europe has slackened its pressure on the world. But the result has been contrary to what might have been expected. Given over to itself, every life has been left empty, with nothing to do. And as it has to be filled with something, it invents frivolities for itself, gives itself to false occupations which impose nothing intimate, sincere. To-day it is one thing, to-morrow another, opposite to the first. Life is lost at finding itself all alone. Mere egoism is a labyrinth. This is quite understandable. Really to live is to be directed towards something, to progress towards a goal. The goal is not my motion, not my life, it is the something to which I put my life and which consequently is outside it, beyond it. If I decide to walk alone inside my own existence, egoistically, I make no progress. I arrive nowhere. I keep turning round and round in the one spot. That is the labyrinth, the road that leads nowhere, which loses itself, through being a mere turning round within itself. Since the war the European has shut himself up within himself, has been left without projects either for himself or for others. Hence we are continuing historically as we were ten years ago.

Command is not exercised in the void. It implies a pressure exercised on others. But it does not imply this alone. If it were only this, it would be mere violence. We must not forget that command has a double effect—someone is commanded, and he is commanded to do something. And in the long run what he is ordered to do is to take his share in an enterprise, in a historic destiny. Hence there is no empire without a programme of life; more precisely, without a programme of imperial life. As the line of Schiller says: "When kings build, the carters have work to do." It will not do, then, to adopt the trivial notion which thinks it sees in the activity of great nations—as of great men—a merely egoistic inspiration. It is not as easy as you imagine to be a pure egoist, and none such have ever succeeded. The apparent egoism of great nations and of great men is the inevitable sternness with which anyone who has his life fixed on some undertaking must bear himself. When we are really going to do something and have dedicated ourselves to a purpose, we cannot be expected to be ready at hand to look after every passer-by and to lend ourselves to every chance display of altruism. One of the things that most delight travellers in Spain is that if they ask someone in the street where such a building or square is, the man asked will often turn aside from his own path and generously sacrifice himself to the stranger, conducting him to the point he is interested in. I am not going to deny that there may be in this disposition of the worthy Spaniard some element of generosity, and I rejoice that the foreigner so interprets his conduct. But I have never, when hearing or reading of this, been able to repress a suspicion: "Was my countryman, when thus questioned, really going anywhere?" Because it might very well be, in many cases, that the Spaniard is going nowhere, has no purpose or mission, but rather goes out into life to see if others' lives can fill his own a little. In many instances I know quite well that my countrymen go out to the street to see if they will come across some stranger to accompany on his way.

It is serious enough that this doubt as to the rule over the world, hitherto held by Europe, should have demoralised the other nations, except those who by reason of their youth are still in their pre-history. But it is still more serious that this marking-time should reach the point of entirely demoralising the European himself. I do not say this because I am a European or something of the sort. I am not saying "If the European is not to rule in the immediate future, I am not interested in the life of the world." Europe's loss of command would not worry me if there were in existence another group of countries capable of taking its place in power and in the direction of the planet. I should not even ask so much. I should be content that no one rule, were it not that this would bring in its train the volatilisation of all the virtues and qualities of European man.

Well, this is what would inevitably happen. If the European grows accustomed not to rule, a generation and a half will be sufficient to bring the old continent, and the whole world along with it, into moral inertia, intellectual sterility, universal barbarism. It is only the illusion of rule, and the discipline of responsibility which it entails, that can keep Western minds in tension. Science, art, technique, and all the rest live on the tonic atmosphere created by the consciousness of authority. If this is lacking, the European will gradually become degraded. Minds will no longer have that radical faith in themselves which impels them, energetic, daring, tenacious, towards the capture of great new ideas in every order of life. The European will inevitably become a day-to-day man. Incapable of creative, specialised effort, he will be always falling back on yesterday, on custom, on routine. He will turn into a commonplace, conventional, empty creature, like the Greeks of the decadence and those of the Byzantine epoch.

A creative life implies a regime of strict mental health, of high conduct, of constant stimulus, which keep active the consciousness of man's dignity. A creative life is energetic life, and this is only possible in one or other of these two situations: either being the one who rules, or finding oneself placed in a world which is ruled by someone in whom we recognise full right to such a function: either I rule or I obey. By obedience I do not mean mere submission—this is degradation—but on the contrary, respect for the ruler and acceptance of his leadership, solidarity with him, an enthusiastic enrolment under his banner.

5

It will be well now to get back again to the starting-point of these articles; to the curious fact that there has been so much talk in these years about the decadence of Europe. It is a surprising detail that this decadence has not been first noticed by outsiders, but that the discovery of it is due to the Europeans themselves. When nobody outside the Old Continent thought of it, there occurred to some men of Germany, England, France, this suggestive idea: "Are we not starting to decay?" The idea has had a good press, and to-day everyone is talking of European decadence as if it were an incontrovertible fact.

But just beckon to the man who is engaged in proclaiming it, and ask him on what concrete, evident data he is basing his diagnosis. At once you will see him make vague gestures, and indulge in that waving of the arms towards the round universe which is characteristic of the shipwrecked. And in truth he does not know what to cling to. The only thing that appears, and that not in great detail, when an attempt is made to define the actual decadence of Europe, is the complex of economic difficulties, which every one of the European nations has to face to-day. But when one proceeds to penetrate a little into the nature of these difficulties, one realises that none of them seriously affect the power to create wealth, and that the Old Continent has passed through much graver crises of this order.

Is it, perhaps, the case that the Germans or the English do not feel themselves to-day capable of producing more things and better things, than ever? Nothing of the kind; and it is most important that we investigate the cause of the real state of mind of Germany or England in the sphere of economics. And it is curious to discover that their undoubted depressed state arises not from the fact that they feel themselves without the capacity; but, on the contrary, that feeling themselves more capable than ever, they run up against certain fatal barriers which prevent them carrying into effect what is quite within their power. Those fatal frontiers of the actual economics of Germany, England, France, are the political frontiers of the respective states. The real difficulty, then, has its roots, not in this or that economic problem which may present itself, but in the fact that the form of public life in which the economic capabilities should develop themselves is altogether inadequate to the magnitude of these latter. To my mind, the feeling of shrinkage, of impotency, which undoubtedly lies heavy on the vitality of Europe in these times is nourished on that disproportion between the great potentialities of Europe and the form of political organisation within which they have to act. The impulse to tackle questions of grave urgency is as vigorous as it has ever been, but it is trammelled in the tiny cages in which it is imprisoned, in the relatively small nations into which up to the present Europe has been organised. The pessimism, the depression, which to-day weighs down the continental mind is similar to that of the bird of widely-spreading wings which, on stretching them out for flight, beats against the bars of its cage.

The proof of this is that the situation is repeated in all the other orders, whose factors are apparently so different from those of economics. Take, for example, intellectual life. Every "intellectual" to-day in Germany, England, or France feels suffocated within the boundaries of his country; feels his nationality as an absolute limitation. The German professor now realises the absurdity of the type of production to which he is forced by his immediate public of German professors, and misses the superior freedom of the French writer or the English essayist. Vice versa, the Parisian man of letters is beginning to understand that an end has come to the tradition of literary mandarinism, of verbal formalism, and would prefer, while keeping some of the better qualities of that tradition, to amplify it with certain virtues of the German professor.

The same thing is happening in the order of internal politics. We have not yet seen a keen analysis of the strange problem of the political life of all the great nations being at such a low ebb. We are told that democratic institutions have lost prestige. But that is precisely what it should be necessary to explain. Because such loss of prestige is very strange. Everywhere Parliament is spoken ill of, but people do not see that in no one of the countries that count is there any attempt at substitution. Nor do even the Utopian outlines exist of other forms of the State which seem, at any rate ideally, preferable. Too much credit, then, is not to be given to the authenticity of this loss of prestige. It is not institutions, *qua* instruments of public life, that are going badly in Europe; it is the tasks on which to employ them. There are lacking programmes of a scope adequate to the effective capacities that life has come to acquire in each European individual. We have here an optical illusion which it is important to correct once for all, for it is painful to listen to the stupidities uttered every hour, with regard to Parliaments, for example. There are a whole series of valid objections to the traditional methods of conducting Parliaments, but if they are taken one by one, it is seen that none of them justifies the conclusion that Parliaments ought to be suppressed, but all, on the contrary, indicate directly and evidently that they should be reformed. Now the best that humanly speaking can be said of anything is that it requires to be reformed, for that fact implies that it is indispensable, and that it is capable of new life. The motor-car of to-day is the result of all the objections that were made against the motor-car of 1910. But the vulgar disesteem into which Parliament has fallen does not arise from such objections. We are told, for example, that it is not effective. Our question should then be, "Not effective for what?" for efficacy is the virtue an instrument possesses to bring about some finality. The finality in this case would be the solution of the public problems of each nation. Hence, we demand of the man who proclaims the inefficacy of Parliaments, that he possess a clear notion of wherein lies the solution of actual public problems. For if not, if in no country is it to-day clear, even theoretically, what it is that has to be done, there is no sense in accusing institutions of being inefficient. It would be better to remind ourselves that no institution in history has created more formidable, more efficient States, than the Parliaments of the XIXth Century. The fact is so indisputable that to forget it implies stark stupidity. We are not, then, to confuse the possibility and the urgency of thoroughly reforming legislative assemblies, in order to render them "even more" efficacious, with an assertion of their inutility.

The loss of prestige by Parliaments has nothing to do with their notorious defects. It proceeds from another cause, entirely foreign to them, considered as political instruments. It arises from the fact that the European does not know in what to utilise them; has lost respect for the traditional aims of public life; in a word, cherishes no illusion about the national States in which he finds himself circumscribed and a prisoner. If this much-talked-of loss of prestige is looked into a little carefully, what is seen is that the citizen no longer feels any respect for his State, either in England, Germany, or France. It would be useless to make a change in the detail of institutions, because it is not these which are unworthy of respect, but the State itself which has become a puny thing.

For the first time, the European, checked in his projects, economic, political, intellectual, by the limits of his own country, feels that those projects—that is to say, his vital possibilities—are out of proportion to the size of the collective body in which he is enclosed. And so he has discovered that to be English, German, or French is to be provincial. He has found out that he is "less" than he was before, for previously the Englishman, the Frenchman, and the German believed, each for himself, that he was the universe. This is, to my mind, the true source of that feeling of decadence which to-day afflicts the European. It is therefore a source which is purely spiritual, and is also paradoxical, inasmuch as the presumption of decadence springs precisely from the fact that his capacities have increased and find themselves limited by an old organisation, within which there is no room for them. To give some support to what I have been saying, let us take any concrete activity; the making of motor-cars, for example. The motor-car is a purely European invention. Nevertheless, to-day, the North-American product is superior. Conclusion: the European motor-car is in decadence. And yet the European manufacturer of motors knows quite well that the superiority of the American product does not arise from any specific virtue possessed by the men overseas, but simply from the fact that the American can offer his product, free from restrictions, to a population of a hundred and twenty millions. Imagine a European factory seeing before it a market composed of all the European States, with their colonies and protectorates. No one doubts that a car designed for five hundred or six hundred million customers would be much better and much cheaper than the Ford. All the virtues peculiar to American technique are, almost of a certainty, effects and not causes of the scope and homogeneity of the market. The "rationalisation" of industry is an automatic consequence of the size of the market.

The real situation of Europe would, then, appear to be this: its long and splendid past has brought it to a new stage of existence where everything has increased; but, at the same time, the institutions surviving from that past are dwarfed and have become an obstacle to expansion. Europe has been built up in the form of small nations. In a way, the idea and the sentiment of nationality have been her most characteristic invention. And now she finds herself obliged to exceed herself. This is the outline of the enormous drama to be staged in the coming years. Will she be able to shake off these survivals, or will she remain for ever their prisoner? Because it has already happened once before in history that a great civilisation has died through not being able to adopt a substitute for its traditional idea of the state.

6

I have recounted elsewhere the sufferings and death of the Graeco-Roman world, and for special details I refer my readers to what is there said.[1] But just now we can take the matter from another point of view.

Greeks and Latins appear in history lodged, like bees in their hives, within cities, *poleis*. This is a simple fact, mysterious in its origin, a fact from which we must start, without more ado, as the zoologist starts from the bald,

[1] *El Espectador*, VI.

unexplained fact that the *sphex* lives a solitary wanderer, whereas the golden bee exists only in hive-building swarms. Excavation and archaeology allow us to see something of what existed on the soil of Athens and Rome before Athens and Rome were there. But the transition from that pre-history, purely rural and without specific character, to the rising-up of the city, a fruit of a new kind produced on the soil of both peninsulas, this remains a secret. We are not even clear about the ethnic link between those prehistoric peoples and these strange communities which introduce into the repertoire of humanity a great innovation: that of building a public square and around it a city, shut in from the fields. For in truth the most accurate definition of the *urbs* and the *polis* is very like the comic definition of a cannon. You take a hole, wrap some steel wire tightly round it, and that's your cannon. So, the *urbs* or the *polis* starts by being an empty space, the *forum*, the *agora*, and all the rest is just a means of fixing that empty space, of limiting its outlines. The *polis* is not primarily a collection of habitable dwellings, but a meeting-place for citizens, a space set apart for public functions. The city is not built, as is the cottage or the *domus*, to shelter from the weather and to propagate the species—these are personal, family concerns—but in order to discuss public affairs. Observe that this signifies nothing less than the invention of a new kind of space, much more new than the space of Einstein. Till then only one space existed, that of the open country, with all the consequences that this involves for the existence of man. The man of the fields is still a sort of vegetable. His existence, all that he feels, thinks, wishes for, preserves the listless drowsiness in which the plant lives. The great civilisations of Asia and Africa were, from this point of view, huge anthropomorphic vegetations. But the Graeco-Roman decides to separate himself from the fields, from "Nature," from the geo-botanic cosmos. How is this possible? How can man withdraw himself from the fields? Where will he go, since the earth is one huge, unbounded field? Quite simple; he will mark off a portion of this field by means of walls, which set up an enclosed, finite space over against amorphous, limitless space. Here you have the public square. It is not, like the house, an "interior" shut in from above, as are the caves which exist in the fields, it is purely and simply the negation of the fields. The square, thanks to the walls which enclose it, is a portion of the countryside which turns its back on the rest, eliminates the rest and sets up in opposition to it. This lesser, rebellious field, which secedes from the limitless one, and keeps to itself, is a space *sui generis*, of the most novel kind, in which man frees himself from the community of the plant and the animal, leaves them outside, and creates an enclosure apart which is purely human, a civil space. Hence Socrates, the great townsman, quintessence of the spirit of the *polis*, can say: "I have nothing to do with the trees of the field, I have to do only with the man of the city." What has ever been known of this by the Hindu, the Persian, the Chinese, or the Egyptian?

Up to the time of Alexander and of Caesar, respectively, the history of Greece and of Rome consists of an incessant struggle between these two spaces: between the rational city and the vegetable country, between the lawgiver and the husbandman, between *jus* and *rus*.

Do not imagine that this origin of the city is an invention of mine, of merely symbolic truth. With strange persistence, the dwellers in the Graeco-Latin city preserve, in the deepest, primary stratum of their memories, this recollection of a *synoikismos*. No need to worry out texts, a simple translation is enough. *Synoikismos* is the resolution to live together; consequently, an assembly, in the strict double sense of the word, physical and juridical. To vegetative dispersion over the countryside succeeds civil concentration within the town. The city is the super-house, the supplanting óf the infra-human abode or nest, the creation of an entity higher and more abstract than the *oikos* of the family. This is the *res publica*, the *politeia*, which is not made up of men and women, but of citizens. A new dimension, not reducible to the primitive one allied to the animal, is offered to human existence, and within it those who were before mere men are going to employ their best energies. In this way comes into being the city, from the first a State.

After a fashion, the whole Mediterranean coast has always displayed a spontaneous tendency towards this State-type. With more or less purity the North of Africa (Carthage = the city) repeats the same phenomenon. Italy did not throw off the City-State till the XIXth Century, and our own East Coast splits up easily into cantonalism, an after-taste of that age-old inspiration.[1]

The City-State, by reason of the relative smallness of its content, allows us to see clearly the specific nature of the State-principle. On the one hand, the word "state" implies that historic forces have reached a condition of equilibrium, of fixedness. In this sense, it connotes the opposite of historic movement: the State is a form of life stabilised, constituted, static in fact. But this note of immobility, of definite, unchanging form, conceals, as does all equilibrium, the dynamism which produced and upholds the State. In a word, it makes us forget that the constituted State is merely the result of a previous move-

[1] It would be interesting to show that in Catalonia there is a collaboration of opposing tendencies: the nationalism of Europe and the *urbanism* of Barcelona, where the tendency of early Mediterranean man survives. I have said elsewhere that our East Coast contains the remnant of *homo antiquus* left in the Peninsula.

ment, of struggles and efforts which tended to its making. The constituted state is preceded by the constituent state, and this is a principle of movement.

By this I mean that the State is not a form of society which man finds ready-made—a gift, but that it needs to be laboriously built up by him. It is not like the horde or tribe or other societies based on consanguinity which Nature takes on itself to form without the collaboration of human effort. On the contrary, the State begins when man strives to escape from the natural society of which he has been made a member by blood. And when we say blood, we might also say any other natural principle: language, for example. In its origins, the State consists of the mixture of races and of tongues. It is the superation of all natural society. It is cross-bred and multilingual.

Thus, the city springs from the reunion of diverse peoples. On the heterogeneous basis of biology it imposes the abstract homogeneous structure of jurisprudence.[1] Of course, this juridical unity is not the aspiration which urges on the creative movement of the State. The impulse is more substantial than mere legality; it is the project of vital enterprises greater than those possible to tiny groups related by blood. In the genesis of every State we see or guess at the figure of a great "company-promoter."

If we study the historical situation immediately preceding the birth of a State, we shall always discover the following lines of development. Various small groups exist, whose social structure is designed so that each may live within itself. The social form of each serves only for an "internal" existence in common. This indicates that in the past they did actually live in isolation, each by itself and for itself, without other than occasional contacts with

---

[1] A juridical homogeneousness which does not necessarily imply centralisation.

its neighbours. But to this effective isolation there has succeeded an "external" common life, above all in the economic sphere. The individual in each group no longer lives only in his own circle, part of his life is linked up with individuals of other groups, with whom he is in commercial or intellectual relations. Hence arises a dis-equilibrium between the two common existences, the "in-ternal" and the "external." Established social forms—laws, customs, religion—favour the internal and make difficult the external which is a newer, ampler existence. In this situation, the State-principle is the movement which tends to annihilate the social forms of internal existence, and to substitute for them a social form adequate to the new life, lived externally. Apply this to actual conditions in Europe, and these abstract expressions will take on form and colour.

There is no possible creation of a State unless the minds of certain peoples are capable of abandoning the tradi-tional structure of one form of common life, and in ad-dition, of thinking out another form not previously exist-ing. That is why it is a genuine creation. The State begins by being absolutely a work of imagination. Imagination is the liberating power possessed by man. A people is capable of becoming a State in the degree in which it is able to imagine. Hence it is, that with all peoples there has been a limit to their evolution in the direction of a State; precisely the limit set by Nature to their imaginations.

The Greek and the Roman, capable of imagining the city which triumphs over the dispersiveness of the coun-tryside, stopped short at the city walls. There were men who attempted to carry Graeco-Roman minds further, to set them free from the city, but it was a vain enterprise. The imaginative limitations of the Roman, represented by Brutus, took in hand the assassination of Caesar, the greatest imagination of antiquity. It is of importance to us Europeans of to-day to recall this story, for ours has reached the same chapter.

7

Of clear heads—what one can call really clear heads—there were probably in the ancient world not more than two: Themistocles and Caesar, two politicians. There were, no doubt, other men who had clear ideas on many matters—philosophers, mathematicians, naturalists. But their clarity was of a scientific order; that is to say, concerned with abstract things. All the matters about which science speaks, whatever the science be, are abstract, and abstract things are always clear. So that the clarity of science is not so much in the heads of scientists as in the matters of which they speak. What is really confused, intricate, is the concrete vital reality, always a unique thing. The man who is capable of steering a clear course through it, who can perceive under the chaos presented by every vital situation the hidden anatomy of the movement, the man, in a word, who does not lose himself in life, that is the man with the really clear head. Take stock of those around you and you will see them wandering about lost through life, like sleep-walkers in the midst of their good or evil fortune, without the slightest suspicion of what is happening to them. You will hear them talk in precise terms about themselves and their surroundings, which would seem to point to them having ideas on the matter. But start to analyse those ideas and you will find that they hardly reflect in any way the reality to which they appear to refer, and if you go deeper you will discover that there is not even an attempt to adjust the ideas to this reality. Quite the contrary: through these notions the individual is trying to cut off any personal vision of reality, of his own very life. For life is at the start a chaos in which one is lost. The individual suspects this, but he is frightened at finding himself face to face with this terrible reality, and tries to cover it over with a curtain of fantasy, where everything is clear. It does not worry him that his "ideas" are not true, he uses them as trenches for the defence of his existence, as scarecrows to frighten away reality.

The man with the clear head is the man who frees himself from those fantastic "ideas" and looks life in the face, realises that everything in it is problematic, and feels himself lost. As this is the simple truth—that to live is to feel oneself lost—he who accepts it has already begun to find himself, to be on firm ground. Instinctively, as do the shipwrecked, he will look round for something to which to cling, and that tragic, ruthless glance, absolutely sincere, because it is a question of his salvation, will cause him to bring order into the chaos of his life. These are the only genuine ideas; the ideas of the shipwrecked. All the rest is rhetoric, posturing, farce. He who does not really feel himself lost, is lost without remission; that is to say, he never finds himself, never comes up against his own reality. This is true in every order, even in science, in spite of science being of its nature an escape from life. (The majority of men of science have given themselves to it through fear of facing life. They are not clear heads; hence their notorious ineptitude in the presence of any concrete situation.) Our scientific ideas are of value to the degree in which we have felt ourselves lost before a question; have seen its problematic nature, and have realised that we cannot find support in received notions, in prescriptions, proverbs, mere words. The man who discovers a new scientific truth has previously had to smash to atoms almost everything he had learnt, and arrives at the new truth with hands bloodstained from the slaughter of a thousand platitudes.

Politics is much more of a reality than science, because
it is made up of unique situations in which a man suddenly finds himself submerged whether he will or no.
Hence it is a test which allows us better to distinguish
who are the clear heads and who are the routineers. Caesar
is the highest example known of the faculty of getting to
the roots of reality in a time of fearful confusion, in one
of the most chaotic periods through which humanity has
passed. And as if Fate had wished to stress still more the
example, she set up, by the side of Caesar's, a magnificent
"intellectual" head, that of Cicero, a man engaged his
whole life long in making things confused. An excess of
good fortune had thrown out of gear the political machinery of Rome. The city by the Tiber, mistress of Italy,
Spain, Northern Africa, the classic and Hellenistic East,
was on the point of falling to pieces. Its public institutions
were municipal in character, inseparable from the city,
like the hamadryads attached under pain of dissolution to
the trees they have in tutelage.

The health of democracies, of whatever type and range,
depends on a wretched technical detail—electoral procedure. All the rest is secondary. If the regime of the elections is successful, if it is in accordance with reality, all goes
well; if not, though the rest progresses beautifully, all
goes wrong. Rome at the beginning of the 1st Century
B.C. is all-powerful, wealthy, with no enemy in front of
her. And yet she is at the point of death because she persists in maintaining a stupid electoral system. An electoral
system is stupid when it is false. Voting had to take place
in the city. Citizens in the country could not take part in
the elections. Still less those who lived scattered over the
whole Roman world. As genuine elections were impossible, it was necessary to falsify them, and the candidates
organised gangs of bravoes from army veterans or circus
athletes, whose business was to intimidate the voters.

Without the support of a genuine suffrage democratic institutions are in the air. Words are things of air, and "the Republic is nothing more than a word." The expression is Caesar's. No magistracy possessed authority. The generals of the Left and of the Right—the Mariuses and the Sullas—harassed one another in empty dictatorships that led to nothing.

Caesar has never expounded his policy, but he busied himself in carrying it out. That policy was Caesar himself, and not the handbook of Caesarism which appears afterwards. There is nothing else for it; if we want to understand that policy, we must simply take Caesar's acts and give them his name. The secret lies in his main exploit: the conquest of the Gauls. To undertake this he had to declare himself in rebellion against the constituted Power. Why? Power was in the hands of the republicans; that is to say the conservatives, those faithful to the City-State. Their politics may be summed up in two clauses. First: the disturbances in the public life of Rome arise from its excessive expansion. The City cannot govern so many nations. Every new conquest is a crime of *lèse-république*. Secondly: to prevent the dissolution of the institutions of the State a *Princeps* is needed. For us the word "prince" has an almost opposite sense to what "princeps" has for a Roman. By it he understood a citizen precisely like the rest, but invested with high powers, in order to regulate the functioning of republican institutions. Cicero in his books, *De Re Publica*, and Sallust in his memorials to Caesar, sum up the thoughts of the politicians by asking for a *princeps civitatis*, a *rector rerum publicarum*, a *moderator*.

Caesar's solution is totally opposed to the Conservative one. He realises that to remedy the results of previous Roman conquests there was no other way than to continue them, accepting to the full this stern destiny. Above all it was necessary to conquer the new peoples of the West, more dangerous in a not-distant future than the effete peoples of the East. Caesar will uphold the necessity of thoroughly romanising the barbarous nations of the West.

It has been said (by Spengler) that the Graeco-Romans were incapable of the notion of time, of looking upon their existence as stretching out into time. They existed for the actual moment. I am inclined to think the diagnosis is inaccurate, or at least that it confuses two things. The Graeco-Roman does suffer an extraordinary blindness as to the future. He does not see it, just as the colour-blind do not see red. But, on the other hand, he lives rooted in the past. Before doing anything *now*, he gives a step backwards, like *Lagartijo*, when preparing to kill.[1] He searches out in the past a model for the present situation, and accoutred with this he plunges into the waves of actuality, protected and disguised by the diving-dress of the past. Hence all his living is, so to speak, a revival. Such is the man of archaic mould, and such the ancients always were. But this does not imply being insensible to time. It simply means an incomplete "chronism"; atrophy of the future, hypertrophy of the past. We Europeans have always gravitated towards the future, and feel that this is the time-dimension of most substance, the one which for us begins with "after" and not "before." It is natural, then, that when we look at Graeco-Roman life, it seems to us "achronic."

This mania for catching hold of everything in the present with the forceps of a past model has been handed on from the man of antiquity to the modern "philologue." The philologue is also blind to the future. He also looks backward, searches for a precedent for every actuality,

[1] The reference is to a well-known bull-fighter, designated, as usual, by his nickname, *The Lizard*.—Tr.

which he calls in his pretty idyllic language, a "source." I say this because even the earliest biographers of Caesar shut themselves out from an understanding of this gigantic figure by supposing that he was attempting to imitate Alexander. The equation was for them inevitable: if Alexander could not sleep through thinking of the laurels of Miltiades, Caesar had necessarily to suffer from insomnia on account of those of Alexander. And so in succession. Always the step backwards, to-day's foot in yesterday's footprint. The modern philologue is an echo of the classical biographer.

To imagine that Caesar aspired to do something in the way Alexander did it—and this is what almost all historians have believed—is definitely to give up trying to understand him. Caesar is very nearly the opposite of Alexander. The idea of a universal kingdom is the one thing that brings them together. But this idea is not Alexander's, it comes from Persia. The image of Alexander would have impelled Caesar towards the East, with its past full of prestige. His decided preference for the West reveals rather the determination to contradict the Macedonian. But besides, it is not merely a universal kingdom that Caesar has in view. His purpose is a deeper one. He wants a Roman empire which does not live on Rome, but on the periphery, on the provinces, and this implies the complete supersession of the City-State. It implies a State in which the most diverse peoples collaborate, in regard to which all feel solidarity. Not a centre which orders, and a periphery which obeys, but an immense social body, in which each element is at the same time an active and a passive subject of the State. Such is the modern State, and such was the fabulous anticipation of Caesar's futurist genius. But this presupposed a power extra-Roman, anti-aristocratic, far above the Republican oligarchy, above its *princeps,* who was merely a *primus inter pares*. That executive power, representative of universal democracy, could only be the Monarchy, with its seat outside Rome. Republic! Monarchy! Two words which in history are constantly changing their *authentic* sense, and which for that reason it is at every moment necessary to reduce to fragments in order to ascertain their actual essence.

Caesar's confidential followers, his most immediate instruments, were not the archaic-minded great ones of the City, they were new men, provincials, energetic and efficient individuals. His real minister was Cornelius Balbus, a man of business from Cadiz, an Atlantic man. But this anticipation of the new State was too advanced; the slow-working minds of Latium could not take such a great leap. The image of the City, with its tangible materialism, prevented the Romans from "seeing" that new organisation of the body politic. How could a State be formed by men who did not live in a City? What new kind of unity was that, so subtle, so mystic as it were? Once again, I repeat: the reality which we call the State is not the spontaneous coming together of men united by ties of blood. The State begins when groups naturally divided find themselves obliged to live in common. This obligation is not of brute force, but implies an impelling purpose, a common task which is set before the dispersed groups. Before all, the State is a plan of action and a programme of collaboration. The men are called upon so that together they may do something. The State is neither consanguinity, nor linguistic unity, nor territorial unity, nor proximity of habitation. It is nothing material, inert, fixed, limited. It is pure dynamism—the will to do something in common—and thanks to this the idea of the State is bounded by no physical limits.

There was much ingenuity in the well-known political emblem of Saavedra Fajardo: an arrow, and beneath it,

"It either rises or falls." That is the State. Not a thing, but a movement. The State is at every moment something which *comes from* and *goes to*. Like every movement, it has its *terminus a quo* and its *terminus ad quem*. If at any point of time the life of a State which is really such be dissected there will be found a link of common life which *seems* to be based on some material attribute or other—blood, language, "natural frontiers." A static interpretation will induce us to say: That is the State. But we soon observe that this human group is doing something in common—conquering other peoples, founding colonies, federating with other States; that is, at every hour it is going beyond what seemed to be the material principle of its unity. This is the *terminus ad quem*, the true State, whose unity consists precisely in superseding any given unity. When there is a stoppage of that impulse towards something further on, the State automatically succumbs, and the unity which previously existed, and seemed to be its physical foundation—race, language, natural frontier—becomes useless; the State breaks up, is dispersed, atomised.

It is only this double aspect of each moment in the State—the unity already existing and the unity in project —which enables us to understand the essence of the national State. We know that there has been as yet no successful definition of a nation, taking the word in its modern acceptation. The City-State was a clear notion, plain to the eyes. But the new type of public unity sprung up amongst Germans and Gauls, the political inspiration of the West, is a much vaguer, fleeting thing. The philologue, the historian of to-day, of his nature an archaiser, feels, in presence of this formidable fact, almost as puzzled as Caesar or Tacitus when they tried to indicate in Roman terminology the nature of those incipient States, transalpine, further Rhine, or Spanish. They called them *civitas, gens, natio*, though realising that none of these names fits the thing.[1] They are not *civitas*, for the simple reason that they are not cities. But it will not even do to leave the term vague and use it to refer to a limited territory. The new peoples change their soil with the greatest ease, or at least they extend or reduce the position they occupy. Neither are they ethnic unities—*gentes, nationes*. However far back we go, the new States appear already formed by groups unconnected by birth. They are combinations of different blood-stocks. What, then, is a nation, if it is neither community of blood nor attachment to the territory, nor anything of this nature?

As always happens, in this case a plain acceptance of facts gives us the key. What is it that is clearly seen when we study the evolution of any "modern nation," France, Spain, Germany? Simply this: what at one period seemed to constitute nationality appears to be denied at a later date. First, the nation seems to be the tribe, and the no-nation the tribe beside it. Then the nation is made up of the two tribes, later it is a region, and later still a county, a duchy or a kingdom. León is a nation but Castile not; then it is León and Castile, but not Aragon. The presence of two principles is evident: one, variable and continually superseded—tribe, region, duchy, king-dom, with its language or dialect; the other, permanent, which leaps freely over all those boundaries and postulates as being in union precisely what the first considered as in radical opposition.

The philologues—this is my name for the people who to-day claim the title of "historians"—play a most de-lightful bit of foolery when, starting from what in our fleeting epoch, the last two or three centuries, the Western nations have been, they go on to suppose that Vercinget-

[1] See Dopsch, *Economic and Social Foundations of European Civilisation*, 2nd ed., 1914, Vol. II, pp. 3, 4.

orix or the Cid Campeador was already struggling for
a France to extend from Saint-Malo to Strasburg, or a
Spain to reach from Finisterre to Gibraltar. These philologues—like the ingenuous playwright—almost always
show their heroes starting out for the Thirty Years' War.
To explain to us how France and Spain were formed, they
suppose that France and Spain pre-existed as unities in
the depths of the French and Spanish soul. As if there
were any French or any Spaniards before France and
Spain came into being! As if the Frenchman and the
Spaniard were not simply things that had to be hammered
out in two thousand years of toil!

The plain truth is that modern nations are merely the
present manifestation of a variable principle, condemned
to perpetual supersession. That principle is not now blood
or language, since the community of blood and language
in France or in Spain has been the effect, not the cause,
of the unification into a State; the principle at the present
time is the "natural frontier." It is all very well for a
diplomatist in his skilled fencing to employ this concept
of natural frontiers, as the *ultima ratio* of his argumenta-
tion. But a historian cannot shelter himself behind it as if
it were a permanent redoubt. It is not permanent, it is not
even sufficiently specific.

Let us not forget what is, strictly stated, the question.
We are trying to find out what is the national State—
what to-day we call a nation—as distinct from other
types of State, like the City-State, or to go to the other
extreme, like the Empire founded by Augustus.[1] If we

---

[1] It is well known that the Empire of Augustus is the *opposite* of
what his adoptive father Caesar aspired to create. Augustus works
along the lines of Pompey, of Caesar's enemies. The best book
on the subject up to the present is E. Meyer's *The Monarchy of
Caesar and the Principate of Pompey* (1918). Though it is the
best, it seems to me greatly insufficient, which is not strange, for
nowhere to-day do we find historians of wide range. Meyer's

want to state the problem still more clearly and concisely, let us put it this way: What real force is it which has produced this living in common of millions of men under a sovereignty of public authority which we know as France, England, Spain, Italy, or Germany? It was not a previous community of blood, for each of those collective bodies has been filled from most heterogeneous blood-streams. Neither was it a linguistic unity, for the peoples to-day brought together under one State spoke, or still speak, different languages. The relative homogeneousness of race and tongue which they to-day enjoy —if it is a matter of enjoyment—is the result of the previous political unification. Consequently, neither blood nor language gives birth to the national State, rather it is the national State which levels down the differences arising from the red globule and the articulated sound. And so it has always happened. Rarely, if ever, has the State coincided with a previous identity of blood and language. Spain is not a national State to-day *because* Spanish is spoken throughout the country,[1] nor were Aragon and Catalonia national States *because* at a certain period, arbitrarily chosen, the territorial bounds of their sovereignty coincided with those of Aragonese or Catalan speech. We should be nearer the truth if, adapting ourselves to the casuistry which every reality offers scope for, we were to incline to this presumption: every lin-

---

book is written in opposition to Mommsen, who was a formidable historian, and although he has some reason for saying that Mommsen idealises Caesar and converts him into a superhuman figure, I think Mommsen saw the essence of Caesar's policy better than Meyer himself. This is not surprising, for Mommsen, besides being a stupendous "philologue," had plenty of the futurist in him. And insight into the past is approximately proportionate to vision of the future.

[1] It is not even true in actual fact that all Spaniards speak Spanish, or all English English, or all Germans High-German.

guistic unity which embraces a territory of any extent
is almost sure to be a precipitate of some previous political
unification.[1] The State has always been the great drago-
man.

This has been clear for a long time past, which makes
more strange the obstinate persistence in considering
blood and language as the foundations of nationality.
In such a notion I see as much ingratitude as inconsist-
ency. For the Frenchman owes his actual France and the
Spaniard his actual Spain to a principle X, the impulse
of which was directed precisely to superseding the narrow community based on blood and language. So that,
in such a view, France and Spain would consist to-day
of the very opposite to what made them possible.

A similar misconception arises when an attempt is made
to base the idea of a nation on a territorial shape, finding the principle of unity which blood and language do
not furnish, in the geographical mysticism of "natural
frontiers." We are faced with the same optical illusion.
The hazard of actual circumstances shows us so-called
nations installed in wide lands on the continent or adjacent
islands. It is thought to make of those actual boundaries
something permanent and spiritual. They are, we are
told, natural frontiers, and by their "naturalness" is implied some sort of magic predetermination of history by
terrestrial form. But this myth immediately disappears
when submitted to the same reasoning which invalidated
community of blood and language as originators of the
nation. Here again, if we go back a few centuries, we
find France and Spain dissociated in lesser nations, with
their inevitable "natural frontiers." The mountain frontier
may be less imposing than the Pyrenees or the Alps, the

---

[1] Account is not taken, of course, of such cases as *Koinón* and
lingua franca, which are not national, but specifically international,
languages.

barrier of water less considerable than the Rhine, the English Channel, or the Straits of Gibraltar. But this only proves that the "naturalness" of the frontiers is merely relative. It depends on the economic and warlike resources of the period.

The historic reality of this famous "natural frontier" lies simply in its being an obstacle to the expansion of people A over people B. Because it is an obstacle—to existence in common or to warlike operations—for A it is a defence for B. The idea of "natural frontiers" presupposes, then, as something even more natural than the frontier, the possibility of expansion and unlimited fusion between peoples. It is only a material obstacle that checks this. The frontiers of yesterday and the day before do no appear to us to-day as the foundations of the French or Spanish nation, but the reverse; obstacles which the national idea met with in its process of unification. And notwithstanding this, we are trying to give a definite, fundamental character to the frontiers of to-day, in spite of the fact that new methods of transport and warfare have nullified their effectiveness as obstacles.

What, then, has been the part played by frontiers in the formation of nationalities, since they have not served as a positive foundation? The answer is clear, and is of the highest importance in order to understand the authentic idea behind the national State as contrasted with the City-State. Frontiers have served to consolidate at every stage the political unification already attained. They have not been, therefore, the starting-point of the nation; on the contrary, at the start they were an obstacle, and afterwards, when surmounted, they were a material means for strengthening unity. Exactly the same part is played by race and language. It is not the natural community of either of these which constituted the nation; rather has the national State always found itself, in its efforts towards unification, opposed by the plurality of races and of tongues, as by so many obstacles. Once these have been energetically overcome, a relative unification of races and tongues has been effected, which then served as a consolidation of unity.

There is nothing for it, then, but to remove the traditional misconception attached to the idea of the national State, and to accustom ourselves to consider as fundamental obstacles to nationality precisely those three things in which it was thought to consist. (Of course, in destroying this misconception, it is I who will now appear to be suffering from one.) We must make up our minds to search for the secret of the national State in its specific inspiration as a State, in the policy peculiar to itself, and not in extraneous principles, biological or geographical in character.

Why, after all, was it thought necessary to have recourse to race, language, and territory in order to understand the marvellous fact of modern nationalities? Purely and simply because in these we find a radical intimacy and solidarity between the individual and the public Power that is unknown to the ancient State. In Athens and in Rome, the State was only a few individuals: the rest—slaves, allies, provincials, colonials—were mere subjects. In England, France, Spain, no one has ever been a mere subject of the State, but has always been a participator in it, one with it. The form, above all the juridical form, of this union in and with the State has been very different at different periods. There have been great distinctions of rank and personal status, classes relatively privileged and others relatively unprivileged; but if we seek to interpret the effective reality of the political situation in each period and to re-live its spirit, it becomes evident that each individual felt himself an active subject of the State, a participator and a collaborator.

The State is always, whatever be its form—primitive, ancient, medieval, modern—an invitation issued by one group of men to other human groups to carry out some enterprise in common. That enterprise, be its intermediate processes what they may, consists in the long run in the organisation of a certain type of common life. State and plan of existence, programme of human activity or conduct, these are inseparable terms. The different kinds of State arise from the different ways in which the promoting group enters into collaboration with the *others*. Thus, the ancient State never succeeds in fusing with the *others*. Rome rules and educates the Italians and the provincials, but it does not raise them to union with itself. Even in the city it did not bring about the political fusion of the citizens. Let it not be forgotten that during the Republic Rome was, strictly speaking, two Romes: the Senate and the people. State-unification never got beyond a mere setting up of communication between groups which remained strangers one to the other. Hence it was that the Empire, when threatened, could not count on the patriotism of the *others*, and had to defend itself exclusively by bureaucratic measures of administration and warfare.

This incapacity of every Greek and Roman group to fuse with other groups arose from profound causes which this is not the place to examine, but which may definitely be summed up in one: the man of the ancient world interpreted the collaboration in which the State inevitably consists, in a simple, elemental, rough fashion, namely, as a duality of governors and governed.[1] It was for Rome

[1] This is confirmed by what at first sight seems to contradict it: the granting of citizenship to all the inhabitants of the Empire. But it turns out that this concession was made precisely when it was losing the character of political status and changing into mere burden and service to the State, or into mere title in civil law. Nothing else could be expected from a State in which slavery was

to command and not to obey; for the rest, to obey and not to command. In this way the State is materialised within the *pomoerium*, the urban body physically limited by walls. But the new peoples bring in a less material interpretation of the State. Since it is a plan of a common enterprise, its reality is purely dynamic; something to be done, the community in action. On this view everyone forms a part of the State, is a political subject who gives his support to the enterprise; race, blood, geographical position, social class—all these take a secondary place. It is not the community of the past which is traditional, immemorial—in a word, fatal and unchangeable—which confers a title to this political fellowship, but the community of the future with its definite plan of action. Not what we were yesterday, but what we are going to be to-morrow, joins us together in the State. Hence the ease with which political unity in the West leaps over all the limits which shut in the ancient State. For the European, as contrasted with the *homo antiquus*, behaves like a man facing the future, living consciously in it, and from its view-point deciding on his present conduct.

Such a political tendency will advance inevitably towards still ampler unifications, there being nothing in principle to impede it. The capacity for fusion is unlimited. Not only the fusion of one people with another, but what is still more characteristic of the national State: the fusion of all social classes within each political body. In proportion as the nation extends, territorially and ethnically, the internal collaboration becomes more unified. The national State is in its very roots democratic, in a sense much more decisive than all the differences in forms of government.

It is curious to observe that when defining the nation

accepted as a principle. For our "nations," on the other hand, slavery was merely a residual fact.

by basing it on community in the past, people always end by accepting as the best the formula of Renan, simply because in it there is added to blood, language and common traditions, a new attribute when we are told that it is a "daily plebiscite." But is the meaning of this expression clearly understood? Can we not now give it a connotation of opposite sign to that suggested by Renan, and yet a much truer one?

8

"To have common glories in the past, a common will in the present; to have done great things together; to wish to do greater; these are the essential conditions which make up a people. . . . In the past, an inheritance of glories and regrets; in the future, one and the same programme to carry out. . . . The existence of a nation is a daily plebiscite." Such is the well-known definition of Renan. How are we to explain its extraordinary success? No doubt, by reason of the graceful turn of the final phrase. That idea that the nation consists of a "daily plebiscite" operates on us with liberating effect. Blood, language, and common past are static principles, fatal, rigid, inert; they are prisons. If the nation consisted in these and nothing more, it would be something lying behind us, something with which we should have no concern. The nation would be something that one is, not something that one does. There would even be no sense in defending it when attacked.

Whether we like it or not, human life is a constant preoccupation with the future. In this actual moment we are concerned with the one that follows. Hence living is always, ceaselessly, restlessly, a *doing*. Why is it not realised that all *doing* implies bringing something future into effect? Including the case when we give ourselves up to remembering. We recall a memory at this

moment in order to effect something in the moment
following, be it only the pleasure of re-living the past.
This modest secret pleasure presented itself to us a moment ago as a desirable future thing, therefore we "make
remembrance of things past." Let it be clear, then, that
nothing has a sense for man except in as far as it is directed towards the future.[1]

If the nation consisted only in past and present, no
one would be concerned with defending it against an
attack. Those who maintain the contrary are either hypo-
crites or lunatics. But what happens is that the national
past projects its attractions—real or imaginary—into the
future. A future in which our nation continues to exist
seems desirable. That is why we mobilise in its defence,
not on account of blood or language or common past. In
defending the nation we are defending our to-morrows,
not our yesterdays.

[1] On this view, the human being has inevitably a futuristic constitution; that is to say, he lives primarily in the future and for
the future. Nevertheless, I have contrasted ancient man with European man, by saying that the former is relatively closed against the
future, the latter relatively open to it. There is, then, an apparent
contradiction between the two theses. This appears only when we
forget that man is a being of two aspects: on the one hand, he is
what he really is; on the other, he has ideas of himself which coincide more or less with his authentic reality. Evidently, our ideas,
preferences, desires cannot annul our true being, but they can com-
plicate and modify it. The ancient and the modern are both concerned about the future, but the former submits the future to a past
regime, whereas we grant more autonomy to the future, to the new
as such. This antagonism, not in being, but in preferring, justifies
us qualifying the modern as a futurist and the ancient as an archaiser. It is a revealing fact that hardly does the European awake
and take possession of himself when he begins to call his existence
"the modern period." As is known, "modern" means the new, that
which denies the ancient usage. Already at the end of the XIVth
Century stress was beginning to be laid on *modernity*, precisely
in those questions which most keenly interested the period, and
one hears, for example, of *devotio moderna*, a kind of vanguard of
"mystical theology."

This is what re-echoes through the phrase of Renan; the nation as a splendid programme for the morrow. The plebiscite decides on a future. The fact that in this case the future consists in a continuance of the past does not modify the question in the least; it simply indicates that Renan's definition also is archaic in nature. Consequently, the national State must represent a principle nearer to the pure idea of a State than the ancient *polis* or the "tribe" of the Arabs, limited by blood. In actual fact, the national idea preserves no little element of attachment to the past, to soil, to race; but for that reason it is surprising to observe how there always triumphs in it the spiritual principle of a unification of mankind, based on an alluring programme of existence. More than that, I would say that that ballast of the past, that relative limitation within material principles, have never been and are not now completely spontaneous in the Western soul; they spring from the erudite interpretation given by Romanticism to the idea of the nation. If that XIXth-Century concept of nationality had existed in the Middle Ages, England, France, Spain, Germany would never have been born.[1] For that interpretation confuses what urges on and constitutes a nation with what merely consolidates and preserves it. Let it be said once and for all —it is not patriotism which has made the nations. A belief in the contrary is a proof of that ingenuousness which I have alluded to, and which Renan himself admits into his famous definition. If in order that a nation may exist it is necessary for a group of men to be able to look back upon a common past, then I ask myself what are we to call that same group of men when they were actually living in a present which from the view-point of to-day is a past. Evidently it was necessary for that common exist-

[1] The principle of nationalities is, chronologically, one of the first symptoms of Romanticism—at the end of the XVIIIth Century.

ence to die away, in order that they might be able to say: "We are a nation." Do we not discover here the vice of all the tribe of philologues, of record-searchers, the professional optical defect which prevents them from recognising reality unless it is past? The philologue is one who, to be a philologue, requires the existence of the past. Not so the nation. On the contrary, before it could have a common past, it had to create a common existence, and before creating it, it had to dream it, to desire it, to plan it. And for a nation to exist, it is enough that it have a purpose for the future, even if that purpose remain unfulfilled, end in frustration, as has happened more than once. In such a case we should speak of a nation untimely cut off; Burgundy, for example.

With the peoples of Central and South America, Spain has a past in common, common language, common race; and yet it does not form with them one nation. Why not? There is one thing lacking which, we know, is the essential: a common future. Spain has not known how to invent a collective programme for the future of sufficient interest to attract those biologically related groups. The futurist plebiscite was adverse to Spain, and therefore archives, memories, ancestors, "mother country," were of no avail. Where the former exists, these last serve as forces of consolidation, but nothing more.[1]

I see, then, in the national State a historical structure, plebiscitary in character. All that it appears to be apart from that has a transitory, changing value, represents the content, or the form, or the consolidation which at each moment the plebiscite requires. Renan discovered the magic word, filled with light, which allows us to exam-

[1] We are at present about to assist, as in a laboratory, at a gigantic definitive experiment: we are going to see if England succeeds in maintaining in a sovereign unity of common life the different portions of her Empire, by furnishing them with an attractive programme of existence.

ine, as by cathode rays, the innermost vitals of a nation, composed of these two ingredients: first, a plan of common life with an enterprise in common; secondly, the adhesion of men to that attractive enterprise. This general adhesion gives rise to that internal solidity which distinguishes the national State from the States of antiquity, in which union is brought about and kept up by external pressure of the State on disparate groups, whereas here the vigour of the State proceeds from spontaneous, deep cohesion between the "subjects." In reality, the subjects are now the State, and cannot feel it—this is the new, the marvellous thing, in nationality—as something extraneous to themselves. And yet Renan very nearly annuls the success of his definition by giving to the plebiscite a retrospective element referred to a nation already formed, whose perpetuation it decides upon. I should prefer to change the sign and make it valid for the nation *in statu náscendi*. This is the decisive point of view. For in truth a nation is never formed. In this it differs from other types of State. The nation is always either in the making, or in the unmaking. *Tertium non datur*. It is either winning adherents, or losing them, according as the State does or does not represent at a given time, a vital enterprise.

Hence it would be most instructive to recall the series of unifying enterprises which have successively won enthusiasm from the human groups of the West. It would then be seen that Europeans have lived on these, not only in their public life, but in their most intimate concerns, that they have kept in training, or become flabby, according as there was or was not an enterprise in sight.

Such a study would clearly demonstrate another point. The State-enterprises of the ancients, by the very fact that they did not imply the close adherence of the human groups among whom they were launched; by the very

fact that the State properly so-called was always circumscribed by its necessary limitation—tribe or city—
such enterprises were practically themselves limitless. A
people—Persia, Macedonia, Rome—might reduce to a
unit of sovereignty any and every portion of the planet.
As the unity was not a genuine one, internal and definitive, it remained subject to no conditions other than
the military and administrative efficiency of the con-
queror. But in the West unification into nations has had
to follow an inexorable series of stages. We ought to be
more surprised than we are at the fact that in Europe
there has not been possible any Empire of the extent
reached by those of the Persians, of Alexander and of
Augustus.

The creative process of nations in Europe has always
followed this rhythm:

First movement.—The peculiar Western instinct which
causes the State to be felt as the fusion of various peoples in a unity of political and moral existence, starts by
acting on the groups most proximate geographically,
ethnically, and linguistically. Not that this proximity is
the basis of the nation, but because diversity amongst
neighbours is easier to overcome.

Second movement.—A period of consolidation in which
other peoples outside the new State are regarded as
strangers and more or less enemies. This is the period
when the nationalising process adopts an air of exclu-
siveness, of shutting itself up inside the State; in a word,
what to-day we call *nationalism*. But the fact is that whilst
the *others* are felt *politically* to be strangers and oppo-
nents, there is economic, intellectual, and moral com-
munion with them. Nationalist wars serve to level out the
differences of technical and mental processes. Habitual
enemies gradually become historically homogeneous. Little by little there appears on the horizon the conscious-

ness that those enemy peoples belong to the same human circle as our own State. Nevertheless, they are still looked on as foreigners and hostile.

Third movement.—The State is in the enjoyment of full consolidation. Then the new enterprise offers itself to unite those peoples who yesterday were enemies. The conviction grows that they are akin to us in morals and interests, and that together we form a national group over against other more distant, stranger groups. Here we have the new national idea arrived at maturity.

An example will make clear what I am trying to say. It is the custom to assert that in the time of the Cid [1] Spain (*Spania*) was already a national idea, and to give more weight to the theory it is added that centuries previously St. Isidore was already speaking of "Mother Spain." To my mind, this is a crass error of historical perspective. In the time of the Cid the León-Castile State was in process of formation, and this unity between the two was the national idea of the time, the politically efficacious idea. *Spania*, on the other hand, was a mainly erudite notion; in any case, one of many fruitful notions sown in the West by the Roman Empire. The "Spaniards" had been accustomed to be linked together by Rome in an administrative unity, as a *diocesis* of the Late Empire. But this geographical-administrative notion was a matter of mere acceptation from without, not an inspiration from within, and by no manner of means an aspiration towards the future.

However much reality one may wish to allow to this idea in the XIth Century, it will be recognised that it does not even reach the vigour and precision which the idea of Hellas had for the Greeks of the IVth. And yet, Hellas was never a true national idea. The appropriate historical comparison would be rather this: Hellas was

[1] Rodrigo de Bivar, *ca.* 1040–1099.

for the Greeks of the IVth Century, and *Spania* for the "Spaniards" of the XIth and even of the XIVth, what Europe was for XIXth-Century "Europeans."

This shows us how the attempts to form national unity advance towards their purpose like sounds in a melody. The mere tendency of yesterday will have to wait until to-morrow before taking shape in the final outpouring of national inspirations. But on the other hand it is almost certain that its time will come. There is now coming for *Europeans* the time when Europe can convert itself into a national idea. And it is much less Utopian to believe this to-day than it would have been to prophesy in the XIth Century the unity of Spain. The more faithful the national State of the West remains to its genuine inspiration, the more surely will it perfect itself in a gigantic continental State.

9

Hardly have the nations of the West rounded off their actual form when there begins to arise, around them, as a sort of background—Europe. This is the unifying landscape in which they are to move from the Renaissance onwards, and this European background is made up of the nations themselves which, though unaware of it, are already beginning to withdraw from their bellicose plurality. France, England, Spain, Italy, Germany, fight among themselves, form opposing leagues, and break them only to re-form them afresh. But all this, war as well as peace, is a living together as equals, a thing which neither in peace nor war Rome could ever do with Celtiberian, Gaul, Briton, or German. History has brought out into the foreground the conflicts and, in general, the politics, always the last soil on which the seed of unity springs up; but whilst the fighting was going on in one field, on a hundred others there was trading with the enemy, an

exchange of ideas and forms of art and articles of faith.
One might say that the clash of fighting was only a curtain behind which peace was busily at work, interweaving
the lives of the hostile nations. In each new generation
the souls of men grew more and more alike. To speak
with more exactitude and caution, we might put it this
way: the souls of French and English and Spanish are, and
will be, as different as you like, but they possess the same
psychological architecture; and, above all, they are gradually becoming similar in content. Religion, science, law,
art, social and sentimental values are being shared alike.
Now these are the spiritual things by which man lives.
The homogeneity, then, becomes greater than if the souls
themselves were all cast in identical mould. If we were
to take an inventory of our mental stock to-day—opinions, standards, desires, assumptions—we should discover
that the greater part of it does not come to the Frenchman from France, nor to the Spaniard from Spain, but
from the common European stock. To-day, in fact, we
are more influenced by what is European in us than by
what is special to us as Frenchmen, Spaniards, and so on.
If we were to make in imagination the experiment of
limiting ourselves to living by what is "national" in us,
and if in fancy we could deprive the average Frenchman
of all that he uses, thinks, feels, by reason of the influence
of other sections of the Continent, he would be terror-
stricken at the result. He would see that it was not possible to live merely on his own; that four-fifths of his
spiritual wealth is the common property of Europe.

It is impossible to perceive what else worth while there
is *to be done* by those of us who live on this portion of
the planet but to fulfil the promise implied by the word
Europe during the last four centuries. The only thing opposed to it is the prejudice of the old "nations," the idea
of the nation as based on the past. We are shortly to

see if Europeans are children of Lot's wife who persist in making history with their heads turned backwards. Our reference to Rome, and in general to the man of the ancient world, has served us as a warning; it is very difficult for a certain type of man to abandon the idea of the State which has once entered his head. Happily, the idea of the national State which the European, consciously or not, brought into the world, is not the pedantic idea of the philologues which has been preached to him.

I can now sum up the thesis of this essay. The world to-day is suffering from a grave demoralisation which, amongst other symptoms, manifests itself by an extraordinary rebellion of the masses, and has its origin in the demoralisation of Europe. The causes of this latter are multiple. One of the main is the displacement of the power formerly exercised by our Continent over the rest of the world and over itself. Europe is no longer certain that it rules, nor the rest of the world that it is being ruled. Historic sovereignty finds itself in a state of dispersion. There is no longer a "plenitude of the times," for this supposes a clear, prefixed, unambiguous future, as was that of the XIXth Century. Then men thought they knew what was going to happen to-morrow. But now once more the horizon opens out towards new unknown directions, because it is not known *who* is going to rule, how authority is going to be organised over the world. *Who*, that is to say, what people or group of peoples; consequently, what ethnic type, what ideology, what systems of preferences, standards, vital movements.

No one knows towards what centre human things are going to gravitate in the near future, and hence the life of the world has become scandalously provisional. Everything that to-day is done in public and in private—even in one's inner conscience—is provisional, the only exception being certain portions of certain sciences. He will be a wise man who puts no trust in all that is proclaimed, upheld, essayed, and lauded at the present day. All that will disappear as quickly as it came. All of it, from the mania for physical sports (the mania, not the sports themselves) to political violence; from "new art" to sun-baths at idiotic fashionable watering-places. Nothing of all that has any roots; it is all pure invention, in the bad sense of the word, which makes it equivalent to fickle caprice. It is not a creation based on the solid substratum of life; it is not a genuine impulse or need. In a word, from the point of view of life it is false. We are in presence of the contradiction of a style of living which cultivates sincerity and is at the same time a fraud. There is truth only in an existence which feels its acts as irrevocably necessary. There exists to-day no politician who feels the inevitableness of his policy, and the more extreme his attitudes, the more frivolous, the less inspired by destiny they are. The only life with its roots fixed in earth, the only autochthonous life, is that which is made up of inevitable acts. All the rest, all that it is in our power to take or to leave or to exchange for something else, is mere falsification of life. Life to-day is the fruit of an interregnum, of an empty space between two organisations of historical rule—that which was, that which is to be. For this reason it is essentially provisional. Men do not know what institutions to serve in truth; women do not know what type of men they in truth prefer.

The European cannot live unless embarked upon some great unifying enterprise. When this is lacking, he becomes degraded, grows slack, his soul is paralysed. We have a commencement of this before our eyes to-day. The groups which up to to-day have been known as nations arrived about a century ago at their highest point of expansion. Nothing more can be done with them except lead them to a higher evolution. They are now mere past accumulating all around Europe, weighing it down, imprisoning it. With more vital freedom than ever, we feel that we cannot breathe the air within our nations, because it is a confined air. What was before a nation open to all the winds of heaven, has turned into something provincial, an enclosed space.

Everyone sees the need of a new principle of life. But as always happens in similar crises—some people attempt to save the situation by an artificial intensification of the very principle which has led to decay. This is the meaning of the "nationalist" outburst of recent years. And, I repeat, things have always gone that way. The last flare, the longest; the last sigh, the deepest. On the very eve of their disappearance there is an intensification of frontiers—military and economic.

But all these nationalisms are so many blind alleys. Try to project one into the future and see what happens. There is no outlet that way. Nationalism is always an effort in a direction opposite to that of the principle which creates nations. The former is exclusive in tendency, the latter inclusive. In periods of consolidation, nationalism has a positive value, and is a lofty standard. But in Europe everything is more than consolidated, and nationalism is nothing but a mania, a pretext to escape from the necessity of inventing something new, some great enterprise. Its primitive methods of action and the type of men it exalts reveal abundantly that it is the opposite of a historical creation.

Only the determination to construct a great nation from the group of peoples of the Continent would give new life to the pulses of Europe. She would start to believe in herself again, and automatically to make demands on, to discipline, herself. But the situation is much more difficult than is generally realised. The years are passing and there is the risk that the European will grow accustomed to the lower tone of the existence he is at present living, will get used neither to rule others nor to rule himself. In such a case, all his virtues and higher capacities would vanish into air.

But, as has always happened in the process of nation-forming, the union of Europe is opposed by the conservative classes. This may well mean destruction for them, for to the general danger of Europe becoming definitely demoralised and losing all its historic strength is added another, more concrete and more imminent. When Communism triumphed in Russia, there were many who thought that the whole of the West would be submerged by the Red torrent. I did not share that view; on the contrary I wrote at the time that Russian Communism was a substance not assimilable by the European, a type that has in its history thrown all its efforts and energies in the scale of individualism. Time has passed, and the fearful ones of a while since have recovered their tranquillity. They have recovered their tranquillity precisely at the moment when they might with reason lose it. Because now indeed is the time when victorious, overwhelming Communism may spread over Europe.

This is how it appears to me. Now, just as before, the creed of Russian Communism does not interest or attract Europeans—offers them no tempting future. And not for the trivial reasons that the apostles of Communism—obstinate, unheeding, strangers to fact—are in the habit of alleging. The bourgeois of the West knows quite well, that even without Communism, the days are numbered of the man who lives exclusively on his income and hands it down to his children. It is not this that renders Europe immune to the Russian creed, still less is it fear. The arbitrary bases on which Sorel founded his tactics of violence twenty years ago seem to us stupid enough to-day. The bourgeois is no coward, as Sorel thought, and at the ac-

tual moment is more inclined to violence than the workers. Everybody knows that if Bolshevism triumphed in
Russia, it was because there were in Russia no bourgeois.[1] Fascism, which is a *petit bourgeois* movement,
has shown itself more violent than all the labour movement combined. It is nothing of all this then that prevents the European from flinging himself into Communism, but a much simpler reason. It is that the European does not see in the Communistic organisation an
increase of human happiness.

And still, I repeat, it seems to me quite possible that
in the next few years Europe may grow enthusiastic for
Bolshevism. Not for its own sake, rather in spite of what
it is. Imagine that the "five year plan" pursued with
herculean efforts by the Soviet Government fulfils ex-
pectations and that the economic situation of Russia is
not only restored, but much improved. Whatever the
content of Bolshevism be, it represents a gigantic human
enterprise. In it, men have resolutely embraced a purpose
of reform, and live tensely under the discipline that such
a faith instils into them. If natural forces, so responseless
to the enthusiasms of man, do not bring failure to this
attempt; if they merely give it free scope to act, its wonderful character of a mighty enterprise will light up the
continental horizon as with a new and flaming constella-
tion. If Europe, in the meantime, persists in the ignoble
vegetative existence of these last years, its muscles flabby
for want of exercise, without any plan of a new life,
how will it be able to resist the contaminating influence
of such an astounding enterprise? It is simply a misunder-
standing of the European to expect that he can hear un-
moved that call to new *action* when he has no standard

---

[1] This ought to be enough to convince us once for all that Marxian
Socialism and Bolshevism are two historical phenomena which have
hardly a single common denominator.

of a cause as great to unfurl in opposition. For the sake of serving something that will give a meaning to his existence, it is not impossible that the European may swallow his objections to Communism and feel himself carried away not by the substance of the faith, but by the fervour of conduct it inspires.

To my mind the building-up of Europe into a great national State is the one enterprise that could counterbalance a victory of the "five year plan." Experts in political economy assure us that such a victory has little probability in its favour. But it would be degradation indeed, if anti-Communism were to hope for everything from the material difficulties encountered by its adversary. His failure would then be equivalent to universal defeat of actual man. Communism is an extravagant moral code, but nothing less than a moral code. Does it not seem more worthy and more fruitful to oppose to that Slavonic code, a new European code, the inspiration towards a new programme of life?

15

We Arrive at the Real Question

THIS IS the question: Europe has been left without a moral code. It is not that the mass-man has thrown over an antiquated one in exchange for a new one, but that at the centre of his scheme of life there is precisely the aspiration to live without conforming to any moral code. Do not believe a word you hear from the young when they talk about the "new morality." I absolutely deny that there exists to-day in any corner of the Continent a group inspired by a new *ethos* which shows signs of being a moral code. When people talk of the "new morality" they are merely committing a new immorality and looking for a way of introducing contraband goods.[1] Hence it would be a piece of ingenuousness to accuse the man of to-day of his lack of moral code. The accusation would leave him cold, or rather, would flatter him. Immoralism has become a commonplace, and anybody and everybody boasts of practising it.

If we leave out of question, as has been done in this essay, all those groups which imply survivals from the past—Christians, Idealists, the old Liberals—there will

[1] I do not suppose there are more than two dozen men scattered about the world who can recognise the springing up of what one day may be a new moral code. For that very reason, such men are the least representative of this actual time.

not be found amongst all the representatives of the actual period, a single group whose attitude to life is not limited to believing that it has all the rights and none of the obligations. It is indifferent whether it disguises itself as reactionary or revolutionary; actively or passively, after one or two twists, its state of mind will consist, decisively, in ignoring all obligations, and in feeling itself, without the slightest notion why, possessed of unlimited rights. Whatever be the substance which takes possession of such a soul, it will produce the same result, and will change into a pretext for not conforming to any concrete purpose. If it appears as reactionary or anti-liberal it will be in order to affirm that the salvation of the State gives a right to level down all other standards, and to manhandle one's neighbour, above all if one's neighbour is an outstanding personality. But the same happens if it decides to act the revolutionary; the apparent enthusiasm for the manual worker, for the afflicted and for social justice, serves as a mask to facilitate the refusal of all obligations, such as courtesy, truthfulness and, above all, respect or esteem for superior individuals. I know of quite a few who have entered the ranks of some labour organisation or other merely in order to win for themselves the right to despise intelligence and to avoid paying it any tribute. As regards other kinds of Dictatorship, we have seen only too well how they flatter the mass-man, by trampling on everything that appeared to be above the common level.

This fighting-shy of every obligation partly explains the phenomenon, half ridiculous, half disgraceful, of the setting-up in our days of the platform of "youth" as youth. Perhaps there is no more grotesque spectacle offered by our times. In comic fashion people call themselves "young," because they have heard that youth has more rights than obligations, since it can put off the fulfilment of these latter to the Greek Kalends of maturity.

The youth, as such, has always been considered exempt from *doing* or *having done* actions of importance. He has always lived on credit. It was a sort of false right, half ironic, half affectionate, which the no-longer young conceded to their juniors. But the astounding thing at present is that these take it as an effective right precisely in order to claim for themselves all those other rights which only belong to the man who has already done something.

Though it may appear incredible, "youth" has become a *chantage;* we are in truth living in a time when this adopts two complementary attitudes, violence and carica-ture. One way or the other, the purpose is always the same; that the inferior, the man of the crowd, may feel himself exempt from all submission to superiors.

It will not do, then, to dignify the actual crisis by pre-senting it as the conflict between two moralities, two civilisations, one in decay, the other at its dawn. The mass-man is simply without morality, which is always, in essence, a sentiment of submission to something, a consciousness of service and obligation. But perhaps it is a mistake to say "simply." For it is not merely a ques-tion of this type of creature doing without morality. No, we must not make his task too easy. Morality cannot be eliminated without more ado. What, by a word lacking even in grammar, is called *amorality* is a thing that does not exist. If you are unwilling to submit to any norm, you have, *nolens volens,* to submit to the norm of denying all morality, and this is not amoral, but immoral. It is a nega-tive morality which preserves the empty form of the other. How has it been possible to believe in the amorality of life? Doubtless, because all modern culture and civilisa-tion tend to that conviction. Europe is now reaping the painful results of her spiritual conduct. She has adopted blindly a culture which is magnificent, but has no roots.

In this essay an attempt has been made to sketch a certain type of European, mainly by analysing his behaviour as regards the very civilisation into which he was born. This had to be done because that individual does not represent a new civilisation struggling with a previous one, but a mere negation. Hence it did not serve our purpose to mix up the portrayal of his mind with the great question: What are the radical defects from which modern European culture suffers? For it is evident that in the long run the form of humanity dominant at the present day has its origin in these defects.

This great question must remain outside these pages. Its treatment would require of us to unfold in detail the doctrine of human existence which, like a *leitmotiv*, is interwoven, insinuated, whispered in them. Perhaps, before long, it may be cried aloud.